SKEWED TO THE RIGHT

T0346319

SKEWED TO THE RIGHT

Sport, Mental Health and Vulnerability

Amy Izycky

PHOENIX
PUBLISHING HOUSE
firing the mind

First published in 2021 by
Phoenix Publishing House Ltd
62 Bucknell Road
Bicester
Oxfordshire OX26 2DS

British Library Cataloguing in Publication Data

A C.I.P. for this book is available from the British Library

ISBN-13: 978-1-912691-82-1

Typeset by vPrompt eServices Pvt Ltd, India

Printed in the United Kingdom

www.firingthemind.com

Contents

Acknowledgements   vii

About the author   ix

Introduction. Where it all began   1

Part I
Weight-restricted sport

1. Rowing   13

2. Horse racing   31

Part II
Skewed to the right: Personality traits that help and hinder

3. Masochism   55

4. Obsessionality   73

5. Focus   93

Part III
Skewed to the left?

6. Acceptance   111

Part IV
Vulnerability

7. Injury and retirement   131

Conclusion. Where do we go from here?   153

Index   171

Acknowledgements

First, to all the sportspeople who have taken part in this project, thank you. Without your generous offer to sit down and to spend time with me sharing your personal stories and experiences, this book would not have been possible. I acknowledge that you, too, hope that by sharing your story you may increase understanding and awareness. I hope that I have done your story justice and that I deliver for you.

Next, to Ken Robinson, not only have you provided expert psychoanalytic guidance throughout this project and with my clinical work, you have also supported me personally and held me through the process. A true mentor, thank you.

To Kate Pearce, an incredible editor and wonderful companion throughout the final phases of production. Your input has been invaluable, thank you.

To my good friend and old rowing partner Leah, my personally appointed first set of eyes, still guiding me in the right direction no less! To Dan Martin for sharing his research findings with me and to Pip Griffiths for making sure that no significant neuropsychological blunders were made!

To Luke Stoltman for agreeing to be the star of the cover and for his good-humoured participation in the socially distanced photo shoot.

To Dr Bryan English, Luke Sutton, the Mulligan Brothers, and Dr Zoe Williams for taking the time to review, consider, and provide feedback on the book, offering their support and backing for the project. I'm incredibly grateful.

And finally, to my analyst, without your input, all of this and everything else would not have been possible. Words are not enough to express my gratitude.

About the author

Dr Amy Izycky is a clinical psychologist and a psychodynamic psycho-therapist specialising in neuropsychology. She graduated from Durham University with an honours degree in psychology and a master's of science in developmental psychopathology. She later went on to complete her doctorate in clinical psychology at Newcastle University and more recently completed her postgraduate diploma in clinical neuropsychology at Glasgow University. Dr Izycky has trained with the North of England Association of Psychoanalytic Psychotherapists (NEAPP) to achieve her Psychodynamic Psychotherapy registration. She represented Durham University as a high-performance rower, competing at national level before going on to compete at club level for many years.

Dr Izycky has a well-established private practice in the North-East of England. She specialises in brain injury, sports-related presentations and adjustment to injury and disability. She works with a variety of international and professional sportspeople who present with mental health difficulties and struggle to adjust to injury and retirement. She has written for peer-reviewed journals, academic texts and *The Guardian*.

Where it all began

Never before has a topic been of such interest to the sporting world and the general population. As more and more sports personalities talk about their own mental health difficulties and internal struggles, we are slowly starting to understand more about the psychology of the successful athlete. So far, many sportspeople have written biographies and have attempted to share their stories. This book intends to go one step further where, as a clinical psychologist, psychodynamic psychotherapist, and a sportsperson myself, I have sat down with athletes and had a conversation with them about their difficulties. They have courageously allowed me to explore these difficulties with them, play around with some ideas, and share them with you through a psychological lens. My ultimate aim, and theirs, is to increase awareness and to inspire further conversation and discussion. We hope that you may find enjoyment, compassion, and understanding in their stories.

I was first exposed to the world of high-performance sport at the age of 19. I was a young and vulnerable girl who was trying to develop into adulthood. I was living away from home for the first time and within two months of me leaving home my mother was diagnosed with breast cancer. I was told to stay at university and continue with my studies. I'd given rowing a go during freshers' week, and as the year progressed I was doing well within the world of college rowing. At the end of my first academic year I won my first novice cup and was spotted by the university and GB development coach. I was approached by my college captain and asked if I wanted to go to trials. I was flattered and I went for it.

The next year I was thrust into what an onlooker, most likely, would have perceived to be an obsessive, masochistic, and socially isolated world that, to your average rower, was par for the course. Of most concern was the day when I was invited to consider being a lightweight rower. It became commonplace to watch girls weighing themselves and training multiple times each day, missing meals, taking laxatives and slimming pills, sweat running in bin bags, and sitting in scalding hot baths in hotel rooms throughout the night in an attempt to make the numbers on the scales correct the next morning. I lasted an academic year and after competing at Henley I returned home, soon to find myself in hospital with appendicitis. I recall waking the morning after emergency surgery and being spoken to in a rather stern way by the surgeon. He told me that if I had left it any longer my appendix would have burst and I would have succumbed to more significant complications. He advised that I should not have ignored the pain, something my rowing training had educated me to do and expected me to do in order to perform. My get well soon card from my then boyfriend was brief and suggested that perhaps this might put an end to "all that silly dieting". I returned to university for my final year and decided not to return to rowing.

My story is not extreme, far from it, but I share it with you as part of the journey that led me to writing this book. This was my first exposure to mental health difficulties in high-performance athletes. Even at such a young age, with an untrained eye, I had a sense that something didn't feel comfortable about what I was being exposed to. Almost 18 years on, I now work as a clinical psychologist and psychodynamic psychotherapist with a wide variety of people who are struggling with their mental health, including elite athletes, albeit to a limited amount, for various reasons that we will consider later in this book.

In 2012, within my role as a clinician, in a discussion with a rowing coach, I was informed that within one small university lightweight rowing team multiple girls and boys were presenting with self-harm and eating disorders. I met with these athletes on a clinical basis, yet for some it was too late and physical intervention was required urgently before any thought could be given to their mental health. For others, meeting with a clinical psychologist was not wanted and conflicted with their sporting goals. I was avoided.

The university acknowledged that it had a duty of care to its students and needed to respond to what was happening. I was introduced to a sociologist, who was once a professional footballer. We worked together and proposed two research projects. One was to explore the specific experience and presentation of lightweight rowers and the other to profile a broad range of athletes across all sports at the university. This was to include assessments of personality and mental health. We only received funding to complete the work with the lightweight rowers and so this is what we did. I had to be careful not to be biased by my own experiences of being a lightweight rower and needed to ensure that the methodology we put in place was as open and unbiased as possible. We collected descriptive background information on each athlete and selected a broad range of assessments measuring personality, distress, alexithymia (inability to recognise and describe one's emotions), self-esteem, and eating-disordered behaviour. We both worked hard on a loose interview structure and themed our questions around what the rowers enjoyed, what they found difficult, and what motivated them. I then trained an assistant psychologist to administer the interview, once again to protect from any bias.

The findings were staggering. Out of the sample of eight lightweight rowers (which was 50% of the total lightweight squad), two athletes reported vomiting to control their weight, five reported bingeing to the point that they felt out of control, and one reported the use of laxatives. Three of these eight individuals presented with a combination of binging, vomiting, and excessive use of exercise to lose weight. In short, it is likely that they would have met the criteria for a diagnosis of an eating disorder. On personality assessment, our sample scored the highest on avoidant, obsessive-compulsive, and depressive personality traits with the most selected items on the personality questionnaire being "I am my own worst critic", "I worry a lot", "If others can't do things correctly, I would prefer to do them myself", "I put my work ahead of being with my family or friends or having fun", and "I am critical of others". The interview identified themes of observing others struggling, extreme weight loss practices, discipline and control, the awareness of coaches judging, the awareness of teammates also being rivals, and self-criticism. If an individual was already in treatment for mental health difficulties (which we were aware some of the squad were) we recommended that they talk to their medical professional to seek advice on whether or not it was advisable for them to take part in the research. None of those that took part were already in treatment and hence our results were indicative of the "healthier" athletes in the squad.

We were seemingly faced with a sample of eight athletes where seven met the criteria for referral to an eating disorder service. Yet despite this, at the point of interview, they told us that "I would describe myself as one of the healthiest and happiest lightweights on the team." They also made reference to much more severe weight loss practices in other members of the squad. They were a highly critical, self-reliant group that perceived the need for little support or would struggle to approach their coaching team for help for fear of judgement. Of course, as with any piece of research, there is always much left open to interpretation, but I was concerned with the findings and I was concerned that this small yet informative group seemed to lack insight into the significance of what they were reporting and the extent of their own needs. Within this elite athlete population, where many were GB athletes or triallists, this behaviour seemed culturally acceptable. I am still astounded with the realisation of how, had these athletes not been in the sporting world and were seen at a doctor's surgery presenting with the symptoms they were reporting, they would be referred to mental health services. However, just because these sportsmen and women were expected to perform in weight-restricted sports, their symptoms were seen simply as a necessary means to an end.

Of course, we must be careful not to assign blame to the world of elite sport or weight-restricted sports. We have to consider if those with a predisposition or vulnerability to going on to develop eating difficulties are attracted to the world of weight-restricted sport as it makes eating-disordered behaviour socially acceptable. And, more generally, certain personality traits or vulnerabilities may well be the very reason why many individuals are attracted to their chosen sport. Perhaps sport maintains and even compounds an existing predisposition for some individuals who need an arena that makes their presentation socially acceptable. For the patient who visits the clinic for assistance with anger management, this may be the pro boxer or MMA cage fighter. For the patient who visits the clinic for an eating disorder, this may be the weight-restricted sportsperson such as the jockey and the lightweight rower.

In psychology, our assessments are based on statistical phenomena. You may recall being taught about the normal distribution or bell curve many years ago in school. In short, it's the phenomenon that if you were to draw a graph showing the number of people that present with a certain characteristic, the majority of people would clump together somewhere in the middle, around average. The graph and the numbers would tail out at the two extremes where only a few people would be located. For example, if we look at height, only a few people would sit at one end around 2 foot tall and likewise only a few would sit at the top end around 8 foot tall but the majority would be somewhere in the middle around 5' 7"; hence, if drawn, this would give us our bell curve. I have used the example of height but psychologists administer personality assessments and a similar phenomenon is seen. Only those who sit two standard deviations (in the extremes) away from average would qualify for significant difference or clinical diagnosis (depending upon the assessment). After working with athletes, I have a theory. I believe that on many personality traits such as masochism, obsessionality, perfectionism, and avoidance, athletes score higher than the average member of the population, yet it is this that actually makes them damn good at what they do. If you look at the illustration below, I would suggest that many elite athletes are skewed to the right on a number of traits. This means they are well equipped to adhere obsessionally to a rigorous training regime and their somewhat greater levels of masochism allow them to push through the pain barrier and not to give up as early as many in the "normal" population might.

For the majority, the thought process is very different when experiencing pain during exercise. Instead of thinking "Push through it" they will more likely think, "This is getting a bit much now, I think I'll stop." If you stop at the first sign of pain, you're not going to make a good athlete. Similarly, if you push through too much pain, you're not going to make a good athlete. This slight difference in personality

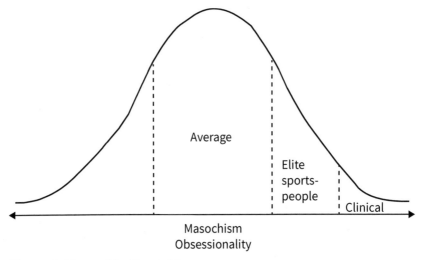

Figure 1 Skewed to the right

structure may be able to distinguish between the average and the elite. If you look at our illustration, however, you may well have already noted that by being skewed to the right on certain personality traits you move closer to the tail end of the curve where we would expect to see our clinical population. Therefore, by the very nature of being skewed on these personality traits, athletes may be more vulnerable to tipping into something that is of clinical significance. In other words, they may present with a clinically diagnosable mental illness. So, in turn, personality traits that help you to be an incredible athlete and may present as socially admirable qualities on the field or on the water—"he has such discipline, such control"—may tip you over into something unhelpful in everyday life.

The first section of the book explores weight-restricted sport and what has become socially acceptable in rowing and horse racing. I discuss with Kieren Emery, retired lightweight GB rower, how his chosen weight-making practices, including "functional vomiting", resulted in significant damage to his body. I then speak with Mark Enright, a professional jockey, who shares his own experiences of a culture whereby weight-control practices, such as sitting in saunas and dehydration, is common practice and widely spoken about. He also talks about his experience of taking Lasix or "piss pills" and the consequences of this. I speak with

Dr Dan Martin, performance nutritionist and researcher, and learn how, despite awareness of an evidence-based diet and exercise plan that will support jockeys to weight reduce and maintain in this healthy way, they are choosing not to. I explore why.

The next section presents a collection of chapters that explore the hypothesis of being skewed to the right. I start by exploring masochism with Michelle Bergstrand, a British cyclo-cross champion, and how experiencing pain becomes something that is habitual and unnoticed, yet satisfies and drives the individual to train and compete. Next, I explore the fine line between healthy and unhealthy obsessionality with Luke Stoltman, Scotland's strongest man, and how obsessions can function to provide control in a world that may be perceived as out of one's control. Finally, with Graeme Fowler, England cricketer, I look at focus. Graeme had developed a strong ability to focus to block out painful things in his past, which served him well in his early life and made him an incredible batsman on the field, allowing him to focus solely on the ball, but which later in life led to significant depression. I then explore the phenomenon of internal acceptance and worth and how conversely, this trait may well be skewed to the left in our elite sports population. In other words, if levels of acceptance and value are lower, this can also drive and motivate sportspeople to perform and achieve. The relationship between acceptance and mental health is explored with Nigel Owens, Welsh international rugby union referee, who talks openly about the impact of his struggles accepting his sexuality and the impact of this on his mental health.

It seems unfortunate that there is a culture of professional sportsmen and sportswomen being idolised and put on a pedestal in the public eye, seemingly with perfect lives. I respect the hard work and sacrifice that goes into becoming a professional sportsperson and I also respect that in our day-to-day lives we need individuals who have achieved and persisted in the face of defeat to inspire and influence us all. I just fear that this need in the general population to idolise our sporting heroes also prevents us from acknowledging their vulnerability and potential difficulties.

I wonder if it is that many athletes are frightened to fall off this pedestal in front of their adoring audiences as they inspire such hope for so many of us. It is no surprise that at times of injury or retirement many of our athletes struggle. My hope in writing this book is not to shatter anyone's beliefs about their sporting hero but instead to enrich their understanding. Perhaps to give the sportsperson some breathing space to acknowledge that they too are human and may also be suffering in some way and may even be more susceptible to suffering because of their greatness and achievements. They should not have to feel that they have to silently present as grateful for what they have achieved. We can still hold them as heroes and hold their great achievements in high esteem as they so deserve, but we may also be able to hold a more balanced view of the person themselves.

The final section of the book dedicates itself to thinking about possible areas of vulnerability for the elite sportsperson. I speak with Jack Rutter, England cerebral palsy football captain, about his struggle through brain injury and his loss of identity as a professional footballer. I explore not only how injury can be a challenge to us all but also why it is that injury and retirement prove to be such a challenge for sportspeople. I explore why it is at retirement when, so very often, we see athletes collapse and struggle with their mental health and what the adjustment process is that must follow for healthy recovery.

We live in a society today that views it fashionable to have a sports psychologist but shaming to have a clinical psychologist. Yet, it is this clinical help that so many of our top athletes need. I am often exposed to professional clubs employing mind coaches with no professional registration and little more than a day's training in stress management or an "alternative" therapy to help athletes through diagnosable clinical difficulties. It is important to understand how both society and the athlete wish to collude with the idea that this is all that is required in an attempt to normalise what they are experiencing, rather than accepting and acknowledging the reality of their mental health.

For many who rely on how they relate to themselves, their body, and their sport to perform at such a high level in order to achieve, it may be incredibly difficult to visit a clinician. I am aware that some have met with me then avoided engaging any further for fear of what exploration and change may bring. Multiple conflicts are inherent in this process and I often feel that many coaches may struggle to send an athlete to a clinician who may work with them on, for example, their obsessionality to help them move closer to a position of health, when it is the very fact that they are so obsessive that makes them an incredible athlete. I often jest with coaches that they do not wish to send their athletes to me in case once they achieve a position of health, they may no longer be motivated to achieve what they have done in the past. I joke but there is also a reality in this. I see it in so many patients. It is important that they themselves are ready before they meet with a clinician or a therapist. We all need our defence mechanisms and we possess them for good reason, because for a certain amount of time they work for us. It is at the point when the individual is able to recognise that this way of being is no longer working that I would encourage them to sit down with a clinician.

A final chapter is dedicated to thinking about how we may change our sports culture to support the next generation of sportspeople. I talk to Ruth Walczak, a GB lightweight rower and then leadership consultant who has specialised in organisational culture change. Ruth concludes that any changes must occur at a systemic level and with consistent messages from all coaching and team staff members. I also talk to Tanni Grey-Thompson, who authored *Duty of Care in Sport: Independent Report to Government*, a review requested by the minister of sport in December 2015. Baroness Grey-Thompson explains how there is a need for a sports ombudsman, along with many other changes, to start to elicit a cultural shift in sport. We also explore the possible barriers to this that include abuse of power and enforced compliance.

In conclusion, I want to acknowledge that I do not wish to suggest that all athletes present with mental health difficulties and/or unhealthy internal drives for engaging in sport, far from it. Some people engage in sport because they just enjoy it! The sporting population is similar to the general population in that it is hetero-geneous in nature and consists of those that have physical health difficulties, mental health difficulties, and those with no difficulties. Hence, this is a reminder that just like the normal population it would be ludicrous to suggest that mental health difficulties do not exist within our sporting populations. If this book is successful in achieving one aim, it is to share with you the stories that have touched me and that I have been privileged to hear and to see, thereby to increase understanding and awareness that even those we idolise, those who are extremely successful in the sporting arena, are just like you and me and that they have stories and histories and very present everyday struggles. I hope that you may understand, may empathise, and may open your eyes that little bit wider.

A note on language use

In each chapter I have interviewed a sportsperson. To ensure that the individual's story and personality is communicated accurately I have decided to include their own words which can frequently include the use of swear words and colloquialisms. I have included clarification in parenthesis for those terms that may be unfamiliar to some readers.

Part I

Weight-restricted sport

CHAPTER 1

Rowing

I thought it best to start my exploration in familiar territory. I was in the car driving to Henley to meet with Kieren Emery, GB lightweight rower. It was the start of July and Henley Royal Regatta was in full motion in its annual slot. I was meeting with Kieren in a house in Henley that he and his rowing team had rented for the entirety of the regatta. In order to get to the house, I found myself driving directly through Henley town. At regatta time, the streets swarm with the wealthy and the "elite". Adorned in boating jackets, they fall off the pavements into the road as if they have right of way over the cars. Brought to a halt at a junction just before the bridge over the river where you can see the finishing tents at Leander rowing club, I sat there, observing. This time, from the safety and containment of my car, I could look from the outside, as someone who 15 years on was now separate from this world. An emotional moment as I acknowledged the state of play in front of me, whereby your boating jacket alone seemingly offered a barometer of your worth and status. Durham University offered seven boating jackets, all offering a differing status dependent upon your rowing achievements. As a senior rower who had competed at Henley and Tideway, I had been given the highest accolade of the palatinate purple blazer with silver trim. If you visit the regatta shop at Henley, if you so desire, you may purchase a rather weighty hardback book for your coffee table that details all the rowing blazers associated to each club so you may identify one's allegiance and status. The traffic lights changed and I drove on to meet with Kieren.

Why do it?

The sacrifice, the pain, and those dark 5 am starts on the river with frost on your shoulders, not to mention the bleeding callouses on your hands that are later doused in white spirit. It begs the question: why do it? Rowing has a reputation as one of the toughest, most demanding sports out there that requires strength, power, and discipline. Perhaps it is the challenge that appeals, and the subsequent glory that may follow if you can master such a beast. Perhaps it is the nature of the sport that appeals to the masochist in so many a sportsperson. Or, what if it were as simple as to say that rowers do it because they enjoy it? Well, I wanted to explore this question. I cannot honestly say that my engagement with the sport was because I enjoyed it 100% of the time, and if you'd have asked me at the time why I was doing it, I don't think I could have answered you. I do not of course wish to suggest that this is the case for everyone, yet in my research project with lightweight rowers, we asked the question, how did you get into rowing? And, more specifically, into lightweight rowing. And what followed was surprising. In short, the entire sample described how it was just something that they stumbled into, something entirely passive. This wasn't a decision these athletes had thought through. They fell into it and then one day they were approached by a coach to see if they wanted to go lightweight. Either for physiological reasons, that is, they were close to the weight required to compete, or they were not competitive enough against the other heavyweights, but, if they lost weight, they had much more chance of being successful.

My first question to Kieren was, "How did you get into the sport?" and what followed shared significant resemblance to my own experience. We had both been noticed by someone who thought we had potential. This, in isolation, was enough. Enough to devote our foreseeable future to the sport. Kieren was found at the age of ten. He told me how he was a bit of a naughty kid off the street and a coach got him by the scruff of the neck and straightened him out. He was not very good at school and was, in Kieren's own words, "a bit of a brat that would cause trouble". He was dyslexic, reading and writing was a big struggle, and most of his friends were not nice people. He is no longer in touch with any of his school friends. He did, however, enjoy rowing because he was good at it. At school he was not good at anything. He was struggling and, at the age of ten, did not understand why. Until his coach and a volunteer at a rowing club—who cooked and looked after many a rower, quickly becoming surrogate mother to many—insisted that Kieren was assessed. He was later diagnosed with dyslexia. In complete contrast to his schooling experience, his coach and the club volunteer sat Kieren down and told him he had potential. It was from this point on, at the age of 16, in 2006, when Kieren started taking rowing seriously.

Like many rowers, Kieren did not start his life as a school rower. It is a generalisation, also largely a reality, that many rowers attend private schools and accessed rowing as a school boy or girl. Kieren came from a working-class family where his mother worked for a local bank and his father was in the Royal Artillery and could be away from home for months at a time. He loved his father but his work meant that it was difficult to sustain a close relationship. Kieren grew up in Germany for the first nine years of his life and then the family moved to a small rural village in the North-East of England. He attended his local school and at the age of ten started to row for his local club. In 2007, at the age of 17, Kieren went to the world championships and told me that he did "OK", he was in the mix of it but was never one of the stand-out competitors. At this time, Kieren had no aspirations to be a GB rower. Instead, he responded with "Oh, I made the team." It was later in his rowing career, when he got a taste for winning, that he wanted it. In 2008, at the age of 18, he won the Junior World Championships in a men's 4+ (a rowing boat consisting of four rowers), enjoyed the feeling and wanted more.

The following year, his coach took Kieren from a mediocre junior to the stand-out junior who won trials by 25 seconds. He won the National Schools regatta, which, in Kieren's words, is a "prestigious preppy school boy event". Later in 2008, Kieren was selected to row in a 4+'s event and came fifth. This was difficult for Kieren as he had worked hard this year and had done worse than the year before. He then struggled with confidence and lost how to race, akin to a mental block. In 2009, Kieren was pulled aside by a different coach who told him that he was not going to make it as a heavyweight but that he really believed he could be a lightweight. He was around the age of 18 or 19 at the time and weighed 84–85 kg. He had never considered being a lightweight rower.

In order to compete in lightweight events, male rowers must weigh in at 75 kg or under during winter season for long distance events and 70 kg or under during summer season for sprint events. Kieren moved down South to compete in GB under-23s and was now living in Henley, rowing for the most prestigious rowing club in the area. Between July and November 2009, Kieren had to drop 10 kg from 85 kg to 75 kg. He did it. Kieren is 6' 2" (1.88 m).

For Kieren, myself, and many rowers that I have spoken to, it never seems to be the plan to get into the sport, let alone to compete at such a high level and as a lightweight. Not only does this apparent passivity in the decision seem to present something of a pattern, it is also the age of this group when they start. It tends to be in the later stages of adolescence when individuals get noticed for rowing. It appears to be the time when physiologically the body settles and coaches can see how tall someone is and how long their limbs are. For rowing, having height and a long arm span are key physiological features. We can therefore consider the individual's physiology as a factor; but what makes an adolescent with no intention of becoming a lightweight rower decide to take this path given the sacrifices that follow?

Well, I would like to introduce the idea of possible existing vulnerability when the individual is noticed, in addition to their physiology. For Kieren, he was a young lad who at school had been given the message that he would never really amount to much; he had not been noticed and selected for academic prowess. At home, Kieren's father had a role where he worked away for much of the time. Developmentally, for boys, having a present male figure who can offer guidance and input on what it is to be a man is important. This doesn't always have to be the father and sometimes may be fulfilled by another relative or someone external to the family. As children, we all need our parents' gaze. It is human nature that we all wish to be noticed and valued and have a place to which to belong. Kieren was potentially struggling to be noticed, for understandable reasons, and then a coach noticed him.

How flattering this must be to a young adolescent's ego. How desirable must it also be, especially for Kieren, when it appeared that he had no other options, to be given an alternative route. He was not achieving at school, he later learnt that he had a diagnosis of dyslexia which would mean his reading and writing would remain challenging, and he was aware that his school friends were a "bad crowd" which he did not wish to be a part of. How do you escape this potential fate in a working-class village in the North-East of England?

When the coach approached Kieren, perhaps his pre-existing vulner-abilities propelled him on an alternative path with a man who demon-strated that he held some belief in Kieren's capabilities and his future. We do not need a psychologist to suggest that for many of our athletes, coaches and other sporting professionals can take on the role of surrogate parents. This dynamic can be magnified if the athlete has lacked something in the past from their own parents. Team this with a coach who has his own developmental experiences that may support the desire to parent or look after vulnerability in others, then a strong bond may be formed. I am not suggesting that this desire is always in one's conscious awareness. In other words, our athletes do not get into sport consciously thinking "I need a replacement father", rather, the guidance and input they receive may feel welcomed and their choices may be guided by their unconscious wishes.

It appears that Kieren's story suggests that the coach and volunteer may have found themselves in a role where they were potentially offering something supportive or parental to a young adolescent who was struggling at school and needed a way out. Kieren told me that he never had a backup plan if he wasn't successful at rowing. He also shared his awareness that the coach went to a private school and did not like the fact that rowing was such a private school boy sport. His coach enjoyed finding new kids and taking them down South to row against the posh school boys and beasting them. It is understandable that a strong relationship formed between this coach and Kieren.

The role of the coach

When Kieren told me about the time in 2009 when he lost his confidence, I asked him if he received much support. To this he spoke about the club volunteer and her husband but then also the coach, telling me that he was a strong male role model. The volunteer and coach clearly provided something for Kieren. They were present for him, they believed in him and his abilities, and they also fought for him. It took the volunteer and the coach to visit his school to complain before he was tested for dyslexia. Even then, testing did not occur and a rowing organisation had to pay to get Kieren assessed after he finished high school. Given Kieren's struggles at school, once he left, he did not have any qualifications. He was certainly not in a position to attend university to study for a degree. His coach therefore supported him to redo his GCSEs at a local college, and in this way he was then able to be coached as part of a university's rowing programme. His coach was, however, "strict" and hammered him every day making sure that he did his work. Kieren is now in a position where he is thinking about going back to university to study for a degree. In the lead-up to this, he has been undertaking additional classes to strengthen his prospects.

If many coaches take on the role of surrogate parent, in reality the parent cannot always be all good and all giving. The parents must also at times disappoint and of course may bring their own agenda or pathology with them into a dynamic. Kieren came to the point in his career where it became all about having to get to the Olympics, to the complete exclusion of anything else in his life. He confirmed that this goal became all-encompassing regardless of how he had to get there. He told me that he did not care about his health or himself and that he also perceived much external pressure. He was aware that his coaches felt he could do it, that he could get to the Olympics, and family and friends would also echo this sentiment. However, internally, Kieren felt that he couldn't. He also was aware of the sacrifices and unhealthy and dangerous eating practices he was engaging in behind closed doors, which none of his coaching team consciously knew of or wished to acknowledge.

While competing at the highest level, Kieren's fat percentage dropped to below 5%. He confirmed that this was unhealthy. He described a scene to me where it was approaching Christmas time and he was looking forward to visiting friends and family. He was now training under a different coaching team. He recalls one lightweight coach from a military background routinely treating Kieren like "one of the troops". On one occasion, the coach told him he had to lose weight over Christmas.

Kieren replied that it was Christmas and he wanted to enjoy himself, to which the coach asserted the same clear message: that he had to lose weight. He returned after Christmas to a training camp abroad where he was "pulled into an office", weighed, and received a telling off. He was told very clearly that he was getting paid to do this. In Kieren's opinion, he was not getting paid enough to do what was expected of him and he was doing it because he wanted to. He responded by saying that he was doing his best and for them not to underestimate this. When Kieren was struggling to make weight, one coach would weigh him every day and would "bollock" him if he put on weight.

I was interested in what Kieren thought about how much awareness the coaching and wider team professionals had with regard to the unhealthy, dangerous eating practices that lightweight athletes may have been engaging in. To this he explained:

> They want a job at the end of the day, it's a business thing. Their job is to create gold medals … keep running on that treadmill, you win a gold medal and the moment you fall off that treadmill they don't care about you.

Kieren felt like a commodity. Once he left competing at a high level, he was no longer covered by his private healthcare nor had access to the team doctors. He had to find his own way with all the physical and psychological consequences from his days as an international rower. As much as he was able to find a supportive coach in his earlier career, as time developed, other coaches presented him with a very different form of support. Perhaps his wish for ongoing care and guidance meant that he stuck on the treadmill for much longer than he would have if he did not present with a pre-existing vulnerability or desire.

Self-reliance

For Kieren, part of his motivation to remain in the sporting world was to find somewhere he belonged, particularly under the support and guidance of containing coaches. For the individual who desires this, it suggests that they are very familiar with having to rely on themselves, typically because of developmental experiences. In my research with a lightweight rower population, I asked them to complete a personality questionnaire and one of the most highly rated items selected to describe themselves was "If I want something doing well I will do it myself". Perhaps a lack of parental presence in the past has led them to become accustomed to fight for themselves. A number of individuals who took part in this research had attended boarding schools before they attended university: an environment where children have to learn to fend for themselves and to adopt a surrogate parent if a professional is willing. This sense of having to fend for oneself may give a lot of athletes the popularised gritty determination or strength required to stay on the treadmill. In part, it appears that this trait could be something that benefits the high-performance athlete. However, it may also be something that hinders them throughout their career and beyond.

When Kieren informed me of the suggestion for him to drop 10 kg to become a lightweight rower, I asked if he received any support to achieve this. He did work with a nutritionist, but ultimately he had to make weight and the suggested plan did not work. He only made weight during the summer of 2010 when he was competing in a lightweight double and at the weigh-in he weighed exactly 70 kg (the maximum he could weigh to compete). It was from this point onwards that Kieren struggled to maintain his weight to support competition as a lightweight.

The eating plan he had been given was not individualised and he felt that this was its downfall. He would have meetings with the nutritionist and would take a food diary. At one point, his food diary documented a daily intake of 1,700 calories and an expenditure of 5,000 calories. This was hard for Kieren; so too was watching friends eat. His social life stopped as a consequence. He would go to bed hungry in an attempt to sleep it off. He got through 2010 and won a silver medal in another lightweight double event. Kieren carried on with this regime, yet from 2011 onwards he started to struggle and things got a "bit unhealthy" as he tried to rely on himself and himself alone to get through the demands of being a lightweight athlete.

Introduction of clinical symptomology

In 2011, Kieren came to weigh-in at a competition and he was overweight by a small amount. He went to the toilets, vomited, and made weight. It was the first time he had made himself sick. From then on, he went through a stage of eating breakfast, enjoying it, and then going to the toilet to throw it back up. Kieren told me that he missed food and he just wanted to eat. The food he would eat was primarily unhealthy food: sweets and ice cream, as ice cream was easy to throw up. This regime seemingly allowed him to still enjoy food but continue to make weight. As he approached the World Championships in 2011, he was doing it more and more. He monitored this rigorously though, weighing himself at least five to six times every day and specifically before eating and then once again after being sick. He would always try to make sure he had returned to his initial weight before eating.

I asked if at any point, when engaging in such methods, did he ever question if the sport was right for him? He explained that he knew, if he were to compete with the heavyweight team he would be at the back of the pack, but with the lightweight team he was in the top three to four athletes and he had a chance of going to the Olympics in London in 2012. So, he did it, but he didn't enjoy it. Competing at the Olympics became the thing that Kieren had to do, regardless of how he got there.

The year of 2011 was a good rowing year for Kieren. He won two World Championship medals but was now regularly inducing vomiting. He is uncertain if he would use the word bulimia to describe what was happening, as when he stopped rowing he stopped vomiting. He was aware that he was miserable and depressed but felt that he was just doing it because it had to be done. What seemed more comfortable to him was using the term "functional vomiting" to describe what he was doing. He was doing it because it had a function and if he wanted to win a gold medal, in his mind, he had to do this.

Bulimia nervosa is diagnosed as follows in the *Diagnostic Statistical Manual* (DSM-5, 2013):

- Recurrent episodes of binge eating. An episode of binge eating is characterised by both of the following:
  - Eating, in a discrete period of time (e.g. within any 2-hour period), an amount of food that is definitely larger than most people would eat during a similar period of time and under similar circumstances.

- ◦ A sense of lack of control over eating during the episode (e.g. a feeling that one cannot stop eating or control what or how much one is eating).
- Recurrent inappropriate compensatory behaviour in order to prevent weight gain, such as self-induced vomiting, misuse of laxatives, diuretics, or other medications, fasting, or excessive exercise.
- The binge eating and inappropriate compensatory behaviours both occur, on average, at least once a week for three months.
- Self-evaluation is unduly influenced by body shape and weight.

Kieren, at that time, met the majority of these criteria, regardless of the fact that his weight concerns were motivated by his sporting endeavours. Concerningly, there was now blood in Kieren's urine and he had to visit a doctor. After having an endoscopy (an investigative procedure where a camera is inserted into the body) he was told that everything was fine. Despite this, he was struggling to continue to make weight, and so continued to make himself sick regularly. At one point, Kieren was in so much kidney pain that he went to his GPs and they injected him with morphine. He then walked out of the doctors and panicked thinking "Oh crap, have I just taken a drug?" He rang another doctor at 11 at night to manage the situation.

I wanted to know if Kieren felt that his professional team knew that he was vomiting regularly and he told me that at the end of his career, some members may have known, but up until that point he had always been very careful. When the team went away on camp, he would always find the toilet furthest away and visit it when he needed to make himself sick. At home, Kieren shared a house with two other people but they each had their own bathrooms and so continuing to vomit was easy. I then asked Kieren if, at the time, he felt that the blood in his urine was connected to his weight-making method of choice and he confirmed that it was. He had visited doctors outside the sport and they were very clear with him that the blood in his urine was a result of malnutrition and how his kidneys and liver were no longer able to function effectively due to his low body weight.

It was then in 2012, when Kieren was in a double at the U23 Worlds that he collapsed after sweating down to make weight. He got back up, told his peers not to say anything, weighed in for the final and drank water. Kieren and his rowing partner won the gold medal in their event. He collapsed a few times but all he could keep thinking in his mind was to "keep going". He believes that the cause of collapse was low blood pressure. Looking back, he thinks his behaviour was stupid and that he should not have pushed himself but at the time he did not see it this way. Instead, he felt that he had gone so far that he had to jump over the last hurdle.

Kieren was not only making himself sick regularly, he was also engaging in other weight-making practices. He would cut out fibre two days before a race and hopefully this would secure a loss of 500 g. He would also sweat down two hours before a race by doing cardiovascular exercise in a sweatsuit. It was surprisingly very quick to lose around 4–5 kg, taking around 45–50 minutes. He would wear five or six pairs of trousers, a hat, scarf and gloves, and get on a rowing machine. The sweat would just drip down his face and when he pulled away at a cuff on his clothes the sweat would fall out. This was, however, in his words, "just being a lightweight" and that every lightweight rower did this. He felt that there were many unhealthy methods that were the cultural norm for lightweight rowers, but he had not spoken to other athletes about this as there was always the fear that the coach may find out and this would have implications for his position in the squad.

Kieren stopped competing as a lightweight rower after London 2012: he got sick and he was pulled out. He had jaundice and glandular fever and was sleeping for 17 hours a day: his body was done.

I interviewed Kieren in the summer of 2017 when his liver and kidneys were in better working order, however his back was not great. He had received multiple injections in his back while rowing and this was seen as par for the course for rowers for all manner of complaints, including slipped discs, bulging discs and/or degenerated discs. Kieren was under no illusion that these injections were just plasters to make sure the athlete was feeling OK to allow them to compete.

In 2011, Kieren came out as gay. Life to Kieren at this time was very challenging. Not only was he struggling with his career and his health, he was struggling to work out who he was. When someone struggles to have a robust sense of who they are, it is very easy for them to conceal certain parts of themselves because these have not yet been integrated.

Secrecy is a key feature in eating disorders and it must be acknowledged that Kieren was bringing this into the dynamic with his team of professionals. I wonder, however, if sometimes this secrecy may be colluded with. Despite a young man of 22 presenting with 5% body fat, blood in his urine, and collapsing multiple times before competing, not one professional in Kieren's recall queried if he had eating difficulties. Why? Perhaps they honestly did not see everything or perhaps they didn't need to query it as it was known but not explicitly acknowledged or spoken about by either party. This scenario begs the question of whose responsibility it is to say something. Kieren was only 22 but he was an adult. He was assessed by internal doctors and external doctors but he was given different opinions. I wonder if for those invested in the sport, there is too much to lose if the truth is acknowledged. Or, perhaps, there has been acclimatisation to the culture that is lightweight sport and clinically diagnosable eating behaviours have become culturally acceptable. These queries are not about attributing blame but are instead an attempt to understand the situation and ensure it does not happen again.

Lack of thinking

Another feature that seems to be ever present in our high-performance population is the lack of thinking in so many of the athlete's actions. For Kieren, when exploring why he started to make himself sick, he told me it was merely done to get the job done. At no stage in his sporting career did he think about his current predicament and health and think "This is no longer working for me." Kieren's career came to an end when his body communicated this to him rather than his mind. It took the dual diagnosis of jaundice and glandular fever. Kieren was then able to say that he did not want to row anymore. He decided to visit America and here he met his husband. He has since moved to the US, works as a rowing coach but is exploring other options, and is very happy.

Perhaps given the extreme sporting practices and associated sacrifices for these athletes, if they were to think about their choices rationally, they would not be able to find any conscious logical reasons to continue to engage with what they are doing. If an athlete is to think, he or she might have to explore the hidden depths behind his or her unconscious motivations for his or her choice. This is tough for anyone to explore if pleasure is not the only reason, especially for someone who is receiving something favourable or positive from what they are doing: yes, I may be engaging in an eating disorder but I could get a gold medal at the Olympics and world recognition. Again, if the individual does not have someone to raise the issue, it is very easy to just keep going without thinking.

While competing at the highest level, Kieren did come into contact with a sports psychologist who was going to do some work with him but Kieren found it too complicated. The sports psychologist made him think about too many things. As Kieren saw it, he just got in a boat and rowed. The sports psychologist wished to explore with Kieren what he should be thinking at the start and the middle of the race, and how he should get to various points in his life. Kieren didn't engage with the sports psychologist. On later reflection, he thinks at that point he was bottling things up and he didn't want anything to come out, so he just kept ploughing on, not thinking about anything.

It is important to clarify the role of a sports psychologist. It is not part of their job to explore clinical difficulties in depth but if such difficulties arise, they should signpost on to a clinical psychologist or registered psychotherapist. If the individual, like Kieren, is not ready, however, then engaging with a sports psychologist, let alone a clinical psychologist, will be challenging. This raises the issue of timing and management for our sporting providers; how best can they support each individual and encourage them to come forward for help? Even if individuals are offered an avenue to explore what is going on, they may not be ready to engage with it. It may well be that sport is serving a very important role to help manage or even defend against difficult times in their life and, at this point, that is enough. Therefore, it is imperative for sports providers to hold a thinking mind and have an awareness of potential vulnerability and need in their athletes that may require support at the right time. This is a much better outlook than simply to collude with the athlete's position of not wanting to think or to know.

Self-esteem and external feedback

For individuals who do not think, or do not have a robust sense of self, their self-worth and value can largely be propped up, intermittently, by external measures in their environment. In the short term, winning gold can show them they are worth something. For individuals whose self-esteem is largely based on external feedback, their self-esteem is a lot more fragile. They are not able to rely on their own internal sense of value regardless of external measures. Remember all those boating jackets lining the streets of Henley and how they instantly assign the individual with their placement within the rowing hierarchy? I spoke with Kieren about this and he told me: "If you don't win a gold medal, you're crap. We're the best in the world, so if you don't win gold, you're just an OK rower."

Kieren had definitely lived a different life to most rowers, especially at the junior level. He recalled going to his first rowing camp and all the other rowers asking him where he went to school. Kieren told them and they did not bother to talk to him afterwards. This fuelled him to kick them all in the arse and make sure he was better than everyone else. He hoped this would result in them coming to him to row with them because he was so good. When he came out as gay, he again wanted to make sure he was the best in the whole team because, then, if they had a problem with him being gay, they would definitely lose and they would lose to a gay guy. For Kieren, it appears that his difference was not something he felt was accepted, be that his working-class background or his sexuality. This fragile sense of self likely challenged Kieren's sense of self-worth and value, and being the best rower meant that others would still need him or want to be around him. I later explore acceptance and worth in more detail in Part III, "Skewed to the left", in discussion with Nigel Owens, Welsh international rugby union referee.

Finding our real self: the reasons why we get into sport

Kieren thought he knew he was gay when he was much younger. However, at that time, he did not feel he had a strong sense of his own mind. He told me how rowing is a macho sport, a very manly sport, and feared that he may lose his friends if he came out. It was in 2012 when Kieren stopped being a lightweight and started rowing as a heavyweight in a quad (4x; a boat that consists of four men who scull with two blades each). He was abroad with his teammates and the only place open was a gay bar. Kieren started talking and dancing with a man inside the bar. His mates pulled him to one side and told him that they loved him. It was after Henley Royal Regatta later that year that more and more people started to learn of Kieren's sexuality and this is when he panicked. He described how he jumped on a plane to New York as he didn't want to be with anyone who knew him. When out in New York, Kieren finally decided to be himself. He felt free to go up to people and tell them who he was and what he did and they didn't care. Whilst out in the States, Kieren was receiving texts from his friends reassuring him that they did not care about his sexuality and that they just wanted him to be a good rower. Kieren is now married to his husband, whom he met in New York during this first visit. All of his friends continue to be supportive. He was able to feel that, for the first time, he could be his true self. He acknowledges that during his rowing years he was hiding. In 2012 he just let it all go and fittingly he described it as "like a whole weight off my shoulders".

Kieren now has a green card and lives in New York with his husband. He feels that he never really thought of the UK as his home and that he fits in over there in the States. He loves his friends and his family but he does not fit in here and he now sees rowing as part of his past life. Kieren does not wish to coach rowing for the rest of his life and is currently exploring other options. He explained that his family were fine with being told about his sexuality; he had anticipated it to be a lot harder. However, he explained that his husband was from a military background and he thinks this helped to adjust his father's perception.

Looking back, Kieren can see his time as a rower for what it is. He also acknowledges that, as part of this process, rowing gave him the "opportunity to be someone, an opportunity to have a better life", that he may not have had if he had not gone down this route.

Anger

Kieren has come out the other side of rowing. He can now see the struggles and the benefits. Despite this, he is left with some under-standable anger towards some of the coaches from later in his rowing career. The management and care of athletes, especially the lightweight athletes, needs to change. Money is ploughed into supporting those athletes performing for their country but not for those who have to leave; a significant factor which can contribute to difficulties adjusting to retirement in sport. Kieren's health is still not great and he still struggles with back pain. As a gold medallist, he was given a grant that totalled less than the annual salary of someone earning minimum wage. Needless to say, Kieren had to work in other jobs to cover his cost of living. The longer-term cost of his physical and mental health difficulties, however, is not measurable.

Summary

Rowing is not alone as a sport that identifies potential athletes when they are young, working with them and shaping them throughout their adolescence. Already, the athlete is at a stage in life when identity is being formed and a desire to find one's own way is inherent. For those adolescents that may present with some isolation and/or a lack of present parenting, the role of the coach in high-performance sports becomes a very powerful one in shaping and influencing the life of the athlete at a suggestible time in their life.

In sport, what is communicated to the adolescent is that external measures and performance attracts the gaze of others and elicits positive feedback—something that a number of more vulnerable athletes may be craving. One's sense of self-worth and value is soon on shaky ground, being influenced primarily by external factors that the athlete can rarely control. This can lead to attempts at excessive controlling behaviour about matters the athlete can influence in order to deliver the desired performance outcome, with some resorting to extreme practices and measures. A dynamic can then be established between coach and athlete, sharing a similar goal, and diffusion of responsibility is inherent when it comes to identifying what is healthy and what is unhealthy for the "adult" athlete. I place "adult" in inverted commas here as I explore in the injury and retirement chapter how emotional development may be somewhat delayed for high-performance athletes, given how the coach inhabits the thinking mind position and the athlete the physical body.

Kieren's story has shed light on cultural norms in lightweight sport, where extreme weight loss methods, which would usually deliver a clinical diagnosis in a visit to the doctor, are denied or labelled as "just being a lightweight". Is it that we are dealing with a denial within sport in order to maintain delivery of results and medals? Or, has a dynamic been established in the group where individuals, coaches and athletes alike have acculturated to practices that are seen as normal? What is happening requires further thought and understanding. So too does the question of who holds the responsibility to not collude with the unhealthy cultural norms. Once these are addressed, it will be possible to start a discussion about change.

CHAPTER 2

Horse racing

I arrived at Mark Enright's home on a drizzly morning on The Curragh an hour outside Dublin and was welcomed in by his partner, Jessie, holding their newborn daughter. Mark was upstairs getting ready as he had been riding that morning. His partner welcomed me warmly into their kitchen and put the kettle on as I sat down at their kitchen table. Mark joined us and in preparation for the interview Jessie placed a plate of chocolate biscuits on the table in front of us. This was not something that I was accustomed to with lightweight athletes. The usual fair consisted of a bottle of water and a polite refusal of any food on the table as "It's alright, I've eaten earlier." I was intrigued to see if Mark would eat a biscuit or if they were for my consumption as special items in the house for a visitor who didn't have to adhere to the strict lightweight regime. As the interview progressed, the biscuits on the table came to represent something much more significant in the world of horse racing and weight management for jockeys. I would soon learn that jockeys do not consider themselves to be a lightweight athlete as the horse is the athlete. The world of weight management for jockeys was not the typical world of weight restriction that I was accustomed to in high-performance sport. Methods for weight restriction were not based on exercise and restricted diet; instead it appeared that they were typically more likely to be based on sweat methods and use of drugs.

Identity

With the exception of being a spectator at horse racing events, I had little insight into the world of professional jockeys. Mark sat with me and explained what it was like. He left school at the age of 16 after completing his junior education certificate in Ireland and moved to Tipperary to sign on as an apprentice with Mick Murphy. It was here that Mark received his apprenticeship licence and a few rides (races) here and there. After a year and a half Mark moved across the road to get a job with Fossey Stack who owned a lot more horses. Here, Mark moved out of home and into a shared house with a couple of other jockeys and at such a young age described how it all went "haywire" for a while. As an apprentice you tend to wake at 7.30 am, ride out the horses, then have lunch at around 1–3 pm. You then return to groom and lead the horses out and then be back home again between 3.30 pm and 5.30 pm. Until 7.30 am the next day he was free to do his own thing. He described how he was in the pub every evening. It was at this point that I recognised something distinctly different to anything I'd ever heard an athlete describe, let alone an athlete that competed in a weight-restricted sport. I had to ask if Mark considered himself to be an athlete. With no hesitation he responded "definitely not". So I asked, it's the horse then that is considered the athlete? "Absolutely," he confirmed. He explained how he has to be fit when he is coming back from an injury and as part of this he may visit the gym or go running to get his strength back, but other than this when he is racing back to back he keeps race fit by racing and riding out. He spoke about friends that were rugby players and an awareness of the hours they put in at the gym and the guilt they feel at eating a biscuit. He spoke of how jockeys were still aware and focused on their weight but their methods were quite different for making race weight. If, on driving home from a race at midnight he weighed 9 stone 11 pounds he might have three pounds to lose for the next day's racing so he would go to McDonalds because he knew he would wake up the same weight as he was the night before. He told me that the theory was that

McDonalds doesn't put any weight on. He wasn't sure why this was the case; he knew it was such a bad choice but "it just runs through you". He explained that the majority of jockeys "eat a lot of shite" with the exception of some flat jockeys (who have to weigh less than jump jockeys) who do struggle with their weight and have to have a good diet. In the main, on the way home from races he told me it was either a McDonalds or Burger King.

Mark described how there is a cultural difference across the jump and flat jockeys: it is more the "city boys" that become involved in flat racing whereas the "bog lads" are more involved in the jumps. He didn't feel that anybody thought less of the jump jockeys but it was just that there is more money in flat racing with bigger prize cheques to be won. This was the first mention of possible hierarchy in the sport. The horses are exceptionally well looked after, they had access to the best physiotherapy, food, and accommodation. At the majority of tracks, Mark explained, jockeys are lucky if they are given a sandwich. He spoke of how the jockeys are "at the end of the scale" and not looked after. This is something that he now sees as just part of the routine in knowing where they stand. He relayed an anecdote where a friend, just six weeks earlier, went to get a biscuit and the young male in charge of catering refused him as they were for the stewards. Race stewards are well looked after and given hot food and pots of tea and biscuits. Mark's friend responded by saying that it was just one biscuit to which the caterer responded that it would cost him 20 cents. Since this incident the Professional Jockeys Association (PJA) have become involved. This has since resulted in free food being available at this particular race course. He described how typically if there are scraps left over at the end of the race meet, like the odd chicken goujon or egg sandwich, these will get put in the changing rooms, almost akin to scraps being thrown in at the end of the day. I was shocked but Mark said that this was just something that they were used to.

As a respected professional jockey Mark is no longer attached to one owner, he is instead self-employed and has established relationships with approximately ten trainers. On a morning he will wake up and ride out one of their horses in hope that they will hold him in mind for forthcoming races. Riding out is not paid for and a jockey is only paid approximately 130 euros per race. If fortunate enough to ride a lot of big winners then the jockey does receive a cut of the prize money after this is taxed. With riding out comes a lot of expenditure, though, as fuel has to be put in the car and miles on the clock are accrued very quickly. At the time of interview, Mark had a car that was only six months old and had 70,000 miles on it. He explained that the TV can portray life for jockeys as an incredible one that includes flash cars and fancy houses, but this is far from the truth. Requests to the jockey for races can be wholly unpredictable.

Disappointment is also par for the course with "no loyalty in the game". Mark described how he could be working his arse off for one trainer who would then call him on Friday night requesting that he races one of his horses for him the next morning. Despite having existing commitments with other trainers the next day Mark would have to disappoint them and cancel racing with them. He explained that it is impossible to keep everyone happy as they all want you at the same time.

He described how, for some jockeys, weight management is a large contributing factor to struggles with mental health, but he also feels that it is the unpredictable nature and the hardship of the sport that can be so challenging. He explained that a lot of jockeys are struggling to make a living and can very quickly be sacked from jobs that they have been booked for if someone better comes along. If you experience a fall and are injured this can also lead to six months out of the sport with no sick pay as a self-employed jockey. Not only this, during this time you can then be forgotten about: trainers don't ring and see how you are doing and other jockeys get your horses.

Expectation to be thick skinned

Mark had experienced multiple injuries over the years, telling me that he had broken most of his bones. In his first few years he had broken his leg, three vertebrae in his back, both wrists, elbow, collarbone, toes, fingers and hands. In the year prior to being interviewed Mark had had three operations. At a race meet at Gowran Park in Ireland he described unbelievably thick fog which left the course unraceable. The stewards came in to see the jockeys and asked them what they thought: the jump jockeys replied that they were happy to ride if the stewards wished them to. Mark told me that the jump jockeys would never say that they don't want to ride as this would make them appear soft, despite it being complete lunacy to go out as they were unable to see in front of them. This was in complete contrast to the flat jockeys who would more than likely not go out. Another time at Roscommon in Ireland, flat jockeys said that the track was slippy whereas the jump jockeys said they would go out anyway. Mark confirmed that he would never say no, especially as jockeys only get paid once they are on the horse's back. He told me that once he had his leg over the horse he got paid.

With this expectation to be thick skinned, one of Mark's biggest challenges came when he returned to the sport after being admitted to hospital with depression for two weeks. He had only told his closest friends and family at the time and his biggest fear was that upon his return to the sport everyone would know and would perceive him to be mad or soft. He recalls asking the lads that he told to not treat him any differently. Initially when Mark was in hospital, Dr Adrian McGoldrick, senior medical officer of the Irish Turf Club, with Mark's agreement, had reported that he was out due to a problem with his appendix. Upon his return, though, Mark had an awareness that news was travelling fast and when entering a changing room he started to feel somewhat paranoid not knowing who knew and who didn't know. Lads would come up and ask him how his appendix was and he didn't want to lie. Mark discussed his thoughts with Adrian and it was agreed that Mark would do a small article with a trusted journalist from the racing post, Jonathon Mullen. Mark went into doing this article with the intention of just sharing the news with people as he didn't want to lie anymore and expected that the piece would be read and then forgotten about. Little did he realise the magnitude of the positive response that he would receive. Since he publicised his struggle with depression and his time on an inpatient mental health unit he has received nothing but thanks, gratitude, and positive feedback. On his first day back, Mark entered the changing room with his head down to which one of the lads cracked a joke and that was the end of it. He then raced and fell at the last fence and got a bollocking from one of the trainers. He had never been so happy, he was being treated no differently.

Despite not labelling himself as an athlete, Mark is not alone in sport in perceiving an expectation to present as tough: in Mark's words, as thick skinned, hardy and as tough as nails. He told me that if you show any sign of weakness you are labelled as "soft … soft as butter". If you break your leg "They want you to walk out the races." I wasn't quite sure who "they" referred to and whether it was an external pressure that he was describing or something that over the years Mark had now come to expect of himself. He went on to tell me, however, that a generational difference is now starting to show. In Galway, Mark recalls cracking his knee cap and receiving physio afterwards. He walked in on crutches and a senior jockey asked what was wrong; when he heard that Mark had cracked his knee cap, he called Mark a "soft whore" because it wasn't broken, telling him, "Shite, you're soft."

With the recent advancement in regulations about head injuries in sport, I wondered if there was a generational difference. Mark explained that he had experienced a couple of head injuries; however, this is something that the sport is very strict on now. Every jockey has to complete baseline assessments of cognition: as soon as they are up off the ground they are asked a string of questions. Mark understood the importance of this, commenting that if he ever sustains a head injury then he would be a danger not only to himself but also to the other 10–15 lads who are in a race with him. At the start, when stricter regulations and guidelines were put in place, some of the jockeys did feel assessment and management was a bit of a pain as they believed that there was nothing wrong with them. There have, however, been a few serious injuries in the last few years which have meant that people respect the guidelines now.

There seems something of a struggle with masculinity and how one identifies as masculine. In the past, to be masculine one should be tough and physically hardy with little show of being capable of being emotional. Things do appear to be changing, however; the challenge now appears to be more about developing one's own voice in sport. Even so, I do wonder how the sport of horse racing adds additional challenges to these men. My first thoughts are of course about size, after all, size is incredibly important for men! Jockeys are required to maintain heights and weights that are closer to the average numbers seen by an adolescent boy. Indeed, the lifestyle at the start of a jockey's career as an apprentice appears to be one where he continues to live the adolescent life, partying and enjoying himself. To make things worse, Mark has increased our awareness of how jockeys are not respected and placed at the bottom of the food chain in their sport, being positioned lower than the horse, stewards, and the owners. How does a jockey gain a robust, stable sense of his place as a man in the world with such significant challenges in his environment? Perhaps having such a reductionist view of what it is to be male—to be as tough as nails—may be protective for the jockey population. The fact that Mark has talked publicly about his experiences with mental health difficulties cannot be underestimated. His ability to be so open about something that may have been perceived in his circles as a weakness is actually one of the greatest displays of a robust sense of masculinity. I did wonder about the timing of Mark's ability to talk about his difficulties and how he met his partner soon afterwards. Perhaps his ability to connect with something in himself opened him up to being more able to connect with another and to be more able to take on the role of a robust husband and then father.

One of the greatest difficulties that I find in the clinic for a lot of young men today is how they can present as males who are respected and valued. Often this leads to a discussion about the differences between aggressiveness, assertiveness, and passivity. Many males strive to be assertive and robust but often struggle, finding themselves locked into an unhelpful pattern of relating aggressively or passively to the world around them. This then of course shapes how people approach them and the dynamic is maintained. I wonder about this in the horse racing world where jockeys can feel like commodities and how difficult it must be to feel respected and valued if you perceive your position in this way. This is not uncommon in many sports and it is the phenomenon that we will explore next.

Being a commodity in a cut-throat world

Mark is now an experienced jockey, he is self-employed and considered to be freelance and not attached to one trainer. Being attached to a stable or a trainer offers jockeys some sense of security. If an owner has 60 horses and three different trainers, a jockey may give two mornings to each trainer. Mark described how on the morning of his interview with me he had been to the Isle of Mead, the following day he was due to be at the Isle of Tipperary, and then he could be on The Curragh the following week. He could be anywhere. Some weeks he could have

15 rides and the next he could have one. This is dependent upon how large the field is, with some races only including five or six horses. Working in this way does not provide a consistent or reliable family income and can be on Mark's mind for much of the time.

At the start of any jockey's career as an apprentice they can make a claim. Each horse that races is given a weight allowance, and if this weight is equal across the field and across the experience of the jockeys the less experienced jockeys can be disadvantaged. To give the apprentices a chance against the more experienced in the field, these less experienced jockeys or conditional jockeys are allowed to claim weight. If a jockey has ridden fewer than 20 winners they can claim up to seven pounds of weight, that is, a horse's weight allowance is reduced by seven pounds. Once a jockey has ridden between 20 and 40 winners a jockey can claim five pounds and then claim three pounds if they have ridden fewer than 75 winners. When he was an apprentice riding out his claim, Mark recalls being told, "Just wait until that claim goes, there will be nothing about you and it will be all about the training of the horse." Mark confirmed this was indeed the case and once he had ridden out his claim, no one wanted to know him. He felt as if everyone was just using him for his claim; even if he had ridden winners for trainers in the past, he wouldn't be used again, and he felt that he was no good to them anymore. There appeared to be no loyalty, he was just a commodity. I wonder what this process communicates to jockeys. I struggled earlier to imagine a sport where the jockey does not consider himself to be an athlete alongside the horse. This lack of respect goes a long way in communicating something consistent with the idea that the jockey is not an athlete. Instead it reduces the jockey's importance to being as light as possible when merely steering the horse. Sadly, this process says little about the skill that the jockey may bring as an athlete with years of experience in his own right.

When he was claiming, Mark was able to make some mistakes as long as he returned and rode a winner. Now, he is aware that he cannot make many mistakes or miss many rides as there are always other lads in front or behind him waiting to step in. Mark could also recognise though that if there was a lad that messed up he could be the one to step in and take his seat. As his career develops in this way, Mark is more and more aware that he has to work harder to continue to get work and to be selected.

With this lifestyle comes much uncertainty and little loyalty. It must also play havoc with the jockey's sense of worth and value. Am I being selected for my racing skills or my claim? Where does a jockey's sense of self, values, and beliefs come into play here when it appears that he is only measured by the number of winners that he has ridden and whether or not he can offer a trainer a claim? Mark confirmed that being dropped can play havoc with his mind. He also spoke of how difficult it is to manage this when he is self-employed. He does not have a team around him such as in football or rugby where players can lean on each other and normalise such feelings. He told me that he is on his own and he has to pull himself together. He explained that he is friends with all the lads on the circuit and that they all try to look after each other as they don't want anyone to get hurt. However, at the end of the day they are all competitors. He explained that he can have four or five lads round for dinner one evening who are then all going into the same place the next day to get a ride. This can of course cause tension. Mark rode a horse last year in the Grand National that his friend had been training on the four or five days before Mark got to know that he was racing it. Mark has thankfully not lost any friendships in this way but it has led to fallings-out that have lasted a couple of weeks. There appeared to be a mutual appreciation of a shared experience by all the jockeys that this isn't easy for anyone.

Keeping others happy; not wanting to disappoint

Unsurprisingly, the unpredictable cut-throat nature of the sport is one of the most challenging things to Mark. He is aware that this can cause him much anxiety. On the night before a race he may have to call round five trainers to let them know that he can no longer race for them. He has an awareness that this will be a disappointment to them and on occasion he can leave it until 10 pm at night thinking about what he is going to say. He isn't going to be able to deliver and he is going to be letting people down. In the past he would be anxious to share this news and then once he had done it he would feel down as he had disappointed people. Mark continues to make every effort to make it up to people on the following day but sometimes this is not possible. When he was younger he just wanted to do everything because he didn't want to let anyone down. He was trying to keep everyone happy and trying to be everywhere. He now realises this is not possible. This appears to be a pre-existing trait from Mark's childhood. He described to me how as a child he would get enjoyment out of making people happy. He recalls small things like getting someone a glass of milk—if he couldn't get it for them he would perceive this as letting them down.

Mark's desire to make others happy has clearly served him well. This is one of the greatest motivators to do well in a race. The hierarchy within racing ensures that Mark is not just wanting to win for himself but for all those that he is working for, for the trainer, for the stable, and for the owner. Like many of the personality traits that are due to be explored in further detail in this book, it is the traits that motivate and help the athlete to be great that can also present as a double-edged sword and can lead to difficulties with mental health. In 2014 Mark started to struggle and had little idea of what was happening to him. Mark was later admitted to a mental health unit.

Depression

Mark felt that the trigger for his depression was the death of an owner, Dessie Hughes, whom he had worked with for a number of years. He described this as a time where there was stability and a structure in his life. On reflection he could, however, identify that up to two years before Dessie's death he was tired all the time and lacked motivation but didn't know what was happening. He described just going through the motions every day and feeling fed up. He could no longer take jokes and would instead find himself getting angry very quickly. Eventually the tiredness got worse and Mark no longer wanted to race as he didn't enjoy what he had loved anymore. In the past he would ride a winner and it would give him a kick. Now, he would ride a winner and it would bring him back to normal. He started to try to find ways to get out of racing—he was sick, he had to go to a funeral—but then he ran out of reasons. He had no interest in people and he would try to avoid everyone. He would leave his phone upstairs, would sit downstairs and be close to panic if it rang. If he didn't see it, it wasn't there.

At this time Mark was living with a few other lads in Kildare; they were younger than him and were regularly out partying until all hours of the morning. They would make noise and Mark would have to go downstairs and clean up in the morning. Dessie then passed away and his daughter took over the horses. She was not an established trainer. She used the best jockeys available and Mark felt pushed out. There was no longer any security to his employment or his daily routine. He became freelance and recalls on New Year's Day going to Tramore with a fellow jockey where he decided he just wasn't going to go back to the house. He recalls having had two falls that day and "not giving a shit what happened". He no longer cared about falling, about the horses, about anything. Mark had had three rides, fell in two and was due to race for a fourth time. He went to see the doctor and said he was too sore. He went home to Killcullen and said to a friend, "Let's go for a pint." Mark didn't return home for four days. He was drinking, fed up of everything, and then he had a breakdown.

Mark didn't know what was going on; he went to a friend's house and they rang Dr McGoldrick. To Mark it felt that the world had ended and he couldn't see a way out. He was so low, in a black hole where there was no way out and everything had gone. Dr McGoldrick sat with Mark for a few minutes while he cried and shook, then he wrote in his notebook, hit Mark on the head and calmly said, "Yep, grand, you're depressed, we'll have you fixed in no time." His calmness has stuck with Mark and to this day he recalls thinking that things couldn't be that bad.

Mark volunteered to spend nearly two weeks in a mental health hospital in Dublin and describes sitting behind the curtain on the ward listening to other people's stories. He didn't interact with anyone but just listened. He thought, "Jesus Christ, I'm not that bad." He saw that his lifestyle was actually quite good and that this was the big kick up the arse that he needed. He still had plenty of bad days after his time in hospital but he was placed on medication and engaged in therapy. He felt that he got to know himself a bit better and learnt how to deal with his struggles. The hospital initially wanted Mark to remain as an inpatient for a month, but given how he is always outdoors he felt that being indoors for this amount of time would be detrimental in itself. In a meeting one week, Mark shared with the team that he liked to be outdoors and that he wanted to leave but that he wanted to continue with therapy. The team agreed to this and Mark left the unit.

Predisposition or creation

Mark started racing at the age of 12 or 13 and left home for the first time at the age of 16. In Chapter One, we explored how coaches can become surrogate parents and it appears that Mark may have found something of this in Dessie. He explained that when he first started out he did want a figure in his life from whom he could receive open feedback on what he was doing wrong and where he could improve. Dessie offered this in the form of a "bollocking" (a slang term for a reprimand) and after he died, there was no one there to pull Mark up. For a long time after that, Mark no longer cared and he didn't want to ride. He told me that a lot of the time, he needs a bollocking. He'll get into a routine and start doing silly things and if there's no one there to stop him, he'll just carry on making mistakes and getting away with them. This loss of a strict parental figure increased Mark's vulnerability to depression. However, as my aim is to develop an understanding of what may predispose sportspeople to difficulties, I wanted to know more about Mark's upbringing.

In therapy, Mark had explored his background and he had remembered that he was never really sad as a child. He wasn't spoiled but he got everything he needed. Yet he could remember being sent into a shop to get Colgate toothpaste. He couldn't find the Colgate and started to panic. Next, he was thinking, "I can't find the fucking Colgate toothpaste," and he went straight into "defence mode" as he called it. He told me that the therapist thought that his difficulties stemmed from this early anxiety. Mark made more sense of it by saying that there has always been something about not wanting to let someone down. If he didn't deliver Colgate toothpaste, he would be letting someone down. As mentioned earlier, to this day he still struggles to ring trainers to cancel.

I was interested in how therapy had supported Mark. He was uncertain what type of therapy he had engaged in, which is not uncommon. I wondered if he had been offered cognitive behavioural therapy (CBT). He described how the therapist would talk about the "what ifs" and how this was Mark's "problem". In other words, he would always think "What if I can't do this?" and, in effect, he was writing himself off before he had even started. The thing he recalled most, though, was not being taught strategies but insight. He got to know himself better and described the experience as "introducing me to myself". At the time of interview Mark feels that he is in a much better place but that he still has bad days. He accepts that everyone has bad days but now he is able to control them a lot better. I wondered how racing has potentially offered Mark an environment where his actions can lead to making a lot of other people happy. The by-product of Mark making weight and riding a horse to a win is the happiness of a lot of other people. It is understandable that Mark gets a kick for various reasons when he wins; however, the flip side of this is how fragile he must be when he does not win and "lets people down" instead of pleasing them.

Mark's story has continued to introduce the idea of pre-existing vulnerability to the development of mental ill health and this will be explored in much more detail in Part II of the book.

Weight management

Initially Mark was a flat jockey; his weight then increased, and he had to compete as a jump jockey. His natural weight, 9 stone 10 lb, now sits around the required 10 stone for a jump jockey. He told me that he eats an "unbelievable amount of shite" and that a lot of the lads are the same. If he has to lose a pound or two he'll sweat it out by running in a sweat suit or by sweating in a sauna. When Mark was a flat jockey and he had to maintain a lower weight of closer to 8 stone, he would resort to more extreme practices. When he was 17 and newly free from home, he was drinking and partying a lot, often having a "chipper" on the way home, and his weight would go up and down repeatedly. On one occasion, he had seven or eight pounds to lose, so he decided to take Lasix, colloquially known as "piss pills". Lasix are a banned substance in racing. Mark told me that they are given to old people in care homes to drain fluids out of their bodies and their joints. Mark was aware they were a banned substance but knew that he had to lose the weight and hoped that they might "get things going". He was young and (in his own words) stupid at the time and he felt in need of a short-term fix. He told me it was useless, however, as even though he lost five pounds, when racing his hips were seizing up, his hands locked, and he could hardly see anything. On this occasion, Mark was drug tested and he received a fine of 1,000 euros.

During the hearing he was asked how many tablets he took, to which he replied, "Two". The turf club doctor told Mark he could have killed himself; patients in care homes receive only half a tablet. Mark had been considering taking six.

I was surprised that Mark had not yet mentioned exercise as a way of managing weight, given my own experience and what Kieren had spoken about when I met with him. I asked Mark about this and he told me that you do not receive a fitness programme when you are a jockey. He is self-employed and weight management is just something he has to do on his own. He told me about a fitness course that he had done with someone last year but that this was to facilitate a return to racing after injury. He explained that primarily jockeys use sweating (running with a sweat suit on or wearing a sweat suit while driving) and diuretics to make weight. Race riding was felt to keep you fit enough. It was with this regime of sweating and the incident with the piss pills that Mark feels he messed up his body and got to a point where he was just too heavy to compete in flat racing anymore. At the time of interview, Mark told me that he does try to eat as healthily as he can now, but he drinks a lot of coffee, being on the road all the time. During the summer when he doesn't leave a race meet until 9.15 pm it tends to be only drive-throughs like McDonalds that are open or a fish and chip shop. He explained that access to food at races for jockeys is not good. Since interviewing Mark, this has now changed, with a new rule being passed in Great Britain by the British Horseracing Authority (BHA) to enforce minimum standards for catering.

Mark doesn't appear to be alone in his relationship to food and exercise and utilising the methods of weight management that he does. He went on to talk about the more extreme end of the spectrum where some young jockeys are now using cocaine. He spoke again of how so many jockeys are so young when they leave home, often living in digs together, free for the first time. Evenings are used to go to the pub as there is nothing else to do after their day's work at the stables. He told me that he has colleagues who have been suspended from racing for six months for use of cocaine and that cocaine is now everywhere. He was encouraged by a friend to sit in a pub and just drink orange juice and watch lads go back and forth to the toilets. He told me that he was shocked with what he saw. Despite random drug tests, cocaine leaves the system after a certain number of days and so doing it on a Saturday night means they know by the next week it will be out of their system. Mark finds the use of cocaine disappointing but feels that part of why the lads are doing it must be related to the fact that they do not identify with being athletes and so do not see the importance of keeping their bodies healthy.

If jockeys do not see themselves as athletes, it is likely that their choice of less than healthy weight management methods must feel acceptable to them. They are not lightweight rowers who are aware that no matter what methods they engage in they are still going to have to try to achieve as close to peak performance as possible. For jockeys, I wonder if it is easier to ignore this external pressure. The horse is the athlete and the object that needs to be in peak health, not the jockey. Sweating and use of pills can of course impact upon the performance of a jockey. Mark explained how after taking piss pills at the start line, jockeys can often feel weak and "virtually useless". It makes me wonder about a jockey's physical and cognitive functioning at this point. At the end of this chapter, I share a discussion that I had with Dr Daniel Martin, a performance nutritionist and researcher who works for the Professional Jockeys Association (PJA), who confirms that dehydration can lead to an increase in the number of falls and deterioration in performance in jockeys, which puts them and everyone else on the field at greater risk.

The start of a cultural shift?

When Mark received his apprentice licence he did a two-week course and recalls the dietician delivering a talk. Mark remembers being told not to drink Red Bull or coffee and not to eat McDonalds. Other than this he was on his own. He now tells me that things are changing. Dr McGoldrick seems to be the catalyst behind this in Ireland. He works across a variety of areas inclusive of weight management and mental health. Now, when a new jockey receives his apprentice licence in Ireland he has to undergo a number of different tests including weight, height, and body fat; he is told what his lowest safe weight is, and he is not allowed to go below this. This is not yet the case throughout Great Britain: jockeys undergo tests but there is no rule in place protecting newly licensed jockeys from taking rides below their minimum weight. It is the work of Dr Jerry Hill, chief medical advisor to the BHA, the PJA, and research conducted at Liverpool John Moores University (LJMU) that is driving change in Great Britain.

Since Mark has spoken publicly about his own struggle with mental health, a 24-hour helpline has been set up for everyone involved in racing. Mark believes that Dr McGoldrick currently has a jockey coming in every week stating that he would welcome support. Mental health now appears to be something that is spoken about in the weighing-in room. This is a huge shift and the PJA is one of the associations that is leading the way with its helpline.

Which psychologist?

The shift that is occurring within horse racing is promising. For all sport, we need to consider what support needs to be provided and how. Mark shared with me that he had met with a sports psychologist. He felt that this would be the thing to give him some motivation. Unfortunately, he found it made things worse for him. He explained that the focus was on performance and he was required to rate his performance on a daily basis. When Mark was struggling, when he felt unmotivated and underperforming, he found this reinforced how bad things were and how much he needed to improve. At the time he felt: "It hit it at the wrong level." He found some "of the little tips good" but said, "It was all about performance, performance, performance and none of it was about me … but if I'm not feeling right in myself then I can't perform."

Mark is helpfully identifying the difference between a sports psychologist and a clinical psychologist. Each has his/her role but what must be identified at the point of need is which professional is going to be the best fit for the athlete. I recall meeting with a sports psychologist at the English Institute for Sport (EIS) some years ago now and we discussed the respective roles of the clinical and sports psychologist. We agreed that what we were dealing with was a diamond model made of two triangles, one upright and one inverted, joined in the middle by a solid platform. If the athlete has a robust platform and is mentally stable when he presents, potentially there is a role for a sports psychologist

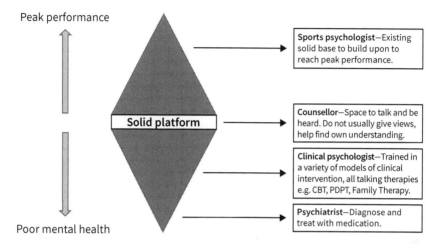

Figure 2 Which professional?

to optimise performance. If an athlete presents with something shakier and they are struggling with their mental health, it is likely that a clinical professional is required and this is where a clinical psychologist would be a good fit.

Mark's comments are very helpful here, with his experience of sports psychology: "It hit it at the wrong level." It reminds us that if the wrong profession becomes involved, it can be harmful. If we are to support sportspeople in the future, the most important first step is that the individual is triaged or assessed by an appropriate professional who is able to identity what the athlete needs. This requires substantial training in itself and should not be taken lightly. An unregulated mindset coach is not qualified for this role and instead a registered sports doctor, sports psychologist or clinical psychologist should be responsible. We then need access to a suitable range of sports and clinical professionals. Finally, we need a change in sporting culture where sportspeople feel able to engage with sports or clinical professionals without fear of judgement and/or loss of respect and position. We can see with the mental health hotline and enhanced training for apprentices in horse racing that some steps are being taken. It is hoped that this book will also increase under-standing and contribute to a cultural shift; however, there is much work still to be done.

How are things changing?

In 2017, I spoke with Dr Dan Martin, performance nutritionist and researcher who works with jockeys. Dan explained that his research has shown that historically there had been no real sports science support for jockeys until the 2010s. It is typical for jockeys to weight cycle (or go up and down with their weight) where they will drop to a really low weight through restriction. Research has found that around 8–15% of jockeys are inducing vomiting. This is happening rather than jockeys engaging in settled weight-making behaviour every day. For flat jockeys in the summer they can be a minimum of 8 stone and for jump jockeys they can weigh a minimum of 10 stone. Physiologically, though, new jockeys entering the industry are getting heavier and taller, specifically 30% heavier than they used to be. Racing has in a positive move increased the minimum weight yet in practice this has only increased by 6% in comparison over the years.

Dr George Wilson, a postdoctoral researcher at LJMU and a colleague of Dr Dan Martin's, has measured weight loss in jockeys and found that what they were losing was water rather than anything more permanent. He responded to this by devising a specific weight loss programme where jockeys would do a 30-minute fasting run before breakfast and then would eat six small meals a day each containing protein. This turned their bodies into fat-burning machines yet what he found was that jockeys were choosing not to implement this. Instead they were continuing to rely on archaic practices such as sweating in saunas and running in sweat suits. Dan's research is currently exploring why they are choosing to do this. He is interviewing jockeys, jockeys' agents and other stakeholders. Using thematic analysis, a qualitative research technique that looks at themes across people's interviews, Dan found that there were a few factors that influence a jockey's decisions. These included a reluctance to change, as what they are doing is not seen as problematic or pathological, it is seen as "the practice". Racing is also role-model-driven: younger jockeys have more experienced idols who they wish to replicate and emulate who engage in these practices and have been successful. Only 20% of those he interviewed would go to see a nutrition expert. The things that are repeatedly said by all jockeys is that they do not like engaging in weight cycling practice but they just do it to make weight: it is seen as a tool in the tool box, as part of the sport and only used when needed. The use of sweating in saunas and diuretics appears to be spoken about freely among jockeys, but although self-induced vomiting occurs it is not spoken about to the same degree.

Just as Mark has spoken about the challenges of being self-employed, Dan also raised the impact of this. He confirmed that if the lads do not ride, they do not get paid and therefore they will do anything to get the work, including challenging weight-making practices. Dan also spoke of a group difference across the jump and flat jockeys. He explained that the flat jockeys tend to be shorter-fused and quick-witted. In his experience he felt flat jockeys appear to have working class backgrounds and routes into racing, with some having no racing family history. He feels that this, along with the greater pressures on diet and weight management contributed to their more edgy demeanour. In contrast, he describes how many jump jockeys arrive as professionals following a background of hunting and point-to-point racing. As a result, they have a different demeanour in how they communicate and, on the whole, seem calmer. Dan suggests the reduced pressure to maintain very low weights plays into this. It is much easier to maintain a 10–11 stone physique than it is an 8–9 stone one. Dan has seen that there does tend to be a difference in attitude to weight practice across these groups. Jump jockeys are more likely to be open to exercise and running whereas the flat jockeys tend more to rely on the use of saunas and vomiting. This does of course seem to make sense, that cultural and educational background would influence attitude towards health and weight management practice.

Another area that Dan is researching is the impact of weight management practice and falls. He spoke of how jockeys have to weigh in and weigh out of races and that they can be sanctioned if they weigh over even after a race. This is not the case for rowing. Anecdotally researchers have queried if jockeys are falling off due to passing out and dehydration. Dan confirmed that there are a few stories of jockeys falling for this reason. He spoke of one in particular where a jockey had lost one stone in a day and fell off halfway round the course. Initially clinicians felt that the jockey had internal bleeding whereas in fact he was near to renal failure given the level of dehydration he was experiencing.

Dan has attempted to replicate dehydration in the lab to explore the impact of this on jockeys. Understandably he and his team have had to be quite careful given the ethical considerations required. They have, however, set up an experiment where they ask jockeys to complete a two-mile race ride on an equiciser and ask them to react to stimuli on the screen in front of them. Ethics would allow them to dehydrate jockeys by 2%. For an 8 stone flat jockey this was only 2 pounds and for a 10 stone jump jockey this was 2½ pounds. They repeated the two-mile race after dehydration and some of the performance markers were down (impaired) by as much as 23%.

Dan feels that there is a lack of nutrition and weight-making education in racing, and while jockey education has improved in recent times, more can be done. Additionally, education for the support entourage that sit around jockeys including agents, trainers, coaches, and racecourse personnel is required given that jockeys are often working to the instruction of these stakeholders. Dan and his colleagues both at the PJA and LJMU are now trying to redress this. It certainly seems that education regarding stable weight-making practice and the impact of dehydration would be very important for jockeys and trainers. It does appear, however, that certain weight practices such as sweating are just seen as part of the job and how things are done. Shifting such a culture that rests on generations of jockeys is going to be incredibly challenging. At the end of this book I invite readers to start to think about how we may begin to elicit a cultural shift in sports that so desperately need it for the health and well-being of their athletes. And here, I am referring to the jockey as the athlete and not just the horse. It is this perception too that needs to change.

Summary

The jockey's world appears to be characterised by isolation and a sense of being bottom of the pile. The jockey is seen as a commodity rather than an athlete. There is an expectation to be thick skinned in a world characterised by hardship and unpredictability. They should fall off, injure themselves, and get back on. Such a world appeared to be a good fit for Mark, who was motivated by wanting to keep everyone happy. This motivated him to achieve and to deliver in the world of horse racing; however, it also left him vulnerable to collapse and depression when he felt he was no longer delivering or when who he was delivering for was no longer in his life.

The horse and its body are respected and treated well, the jockey and his body are not. A cultural way of being has been established. Lack of respect likely influences weight-making practice that can be characterised by "eating shite", use of diuretics, induced vomiting, cocaine, Lasix and sweating. Despite attempts to offer advice and information regarding stable weight-making behaviour, jockeys continue to follow the archaic practices of many generations of jockeys before them. The jockeys' cultural experience of the horse racing world appears to maintain such weight-making practice. If this is to change, the current dynamic of how jockeys are perceived and related to in the sport will need to shift to one where jockeys and their bodies may be respected and responded to more compassionately. Otherwise, we run the risk of the current state of play being maintained.

Part II

Skewed to the right
Personality traits that help and hinder

CHAPTER 3

Masochism

In this chapter, as in all the chapters in this book, interviews with current or ex-professional athletes are shared. As a clinical psychologist and a psychodynamic psychotherapist, I am inevitably interested in people's developmental experiences and family background. And yes, this does include an exploration of their relationship with their mother and father. I am aware that instantly, for many a reader, hackles have just stood up on the back of your neck. Stay with me, as I hope to explain the reality of why we explore these areas. And, how it directly relates to the skewed to the right phenomenon.

There is a popular misconception that psychologists and psychoanalysts wish to blame everything on parents. This is not the case and I wish to offer clarification at the outset. I will be exploring these relationships but not because I am searching for someone to blame or to release the athlete of any personal responsibility. A common misconception is that the exploration of the relationships with parenting figures is about absolving the individual of any personal responsibility or autonomy in their ability to change. However, the reason for exploring these relationships is because ways of being are passed unconsciously through the generations. Part of these unconscious ways of being relate to templates that are laid down from our very early years, and even before conception.

The personality that falls out of these developmental experiences is then the thing that psychologists explore.

I am suggesting that athletes are skewed to the right on a number of personality traits because of their developmental experiences. This unconsciously draws them to ways of maintaining this way of being by continuing to engage in environments, in relationships, or even in a sport that allows them to continue to be obsessive or abusive towards themselves because this is their template way of being. Many of these behaviours are encouraged in the sport environment and are seen as culturally acceptable, and so become normalised. I have written about this already in the weight-restricted section. Again, just as this book is not about blaming parents it is also not about blaming sport in any way. It is about understanding why sport is being used as an object or outlet for some individuals to continue to maintain their template ways of being and how, in turn, this then leaves them vulnerable to developing mental ill health.

Another common misconception is that the reason we like to ask about the past and developmental experiences is because we are searching for a significant trauma or an experience that may have been denied or repressed. Again, this is not the case. It may be the reality for some but certainly not for all and a lack of trauma does not indicate a lack of struggle in life. In psychoanalysis we are looking at much greater complexity and nuance. As part of psychodynamic training we observe a new mother and her newborn baby once a week, from birth through to one year, sometimes older. This first year lays down our templates, our ways of being, what we expect from the world, what we expect from caregivers, what we expect from male figures (typically fathers), and what we expect from female figures (typically mothers). It does not matter that we do not have concrete conscious memories from this age: our unconscious and our bodies remember. We then also have years and years after our first year of life that continue to maintain things for us. And of these things, we do have conscious memories. Later in life our parents teach us about what it is to be a couple and how we must separate into our own way of being as an adult.

I feel that, sadly, psychoanalysis and Freud's theories are lost on so many as they are taken at face value rather than being thought about as they were always intended to be. This was in dealing with processes that are out of our conscious awareness and those that operate on the level of fantasy. My hope is that these interviews and the accompanying commentary will demonstrate that exploration of these early dynamics aids understanding, rather than facilitates blame. Once we understand, we can then start to explore why certain patterns and ways of relating to others are maintained. This can then lead to change. By purely responding to conscious thoughts, the unconscious can continue to trip people up, self-sabotage, and undermine any attempts at change. Later in the book, in the obsessionality chapter, I explore the neuro-psychology of addiction and how changes in the biology of the brain and neurotransmitter pathways associated to addiction can also apply in sport. This then becomes one contributing factor that means behavioural change is so challenging. In other words, just telling yourself to think differently or change your behaviour is not the answer. If only it were that simple. If it were, I doubt we would require the extensive mental health services and variety of treatment modalities that already exist and continue to be developed.

Any information shared with me by the sportspeople in this book has been shared as information that has been perceived by them through their own internal lens. My interpretations and thoughts are based solely on the information they give me. I acknowledge that I have not been able to sit with each of their parents/partners/coaches and so on to explore all perceptions of the same experience. I therefore acknowledge that there will be multiple perspectives on the same story and this book will only share one of those. Given the nature of what this book is exploring, however, and also in keeping with that of therapy, as a clinician, I am only interested in the perception of the client, or in this case the athlete, as it is their story, and their internal world that we are exploring. This is after all what leads to the struggle for the individual. I have, where possible, throughout the book attempted to maintain anonymity. I hope that anyone who may be able to identify themselves understands that this book is only sharing one perspective and, as already highlighted, is not about wishing to assign blame. Instead, it is to aid the understanding of dynamics that are established and maintained between people and groups for a multitude of complex reasons. My aim is to increase social awareness and stimulate thought about how we may learn from these stories and best support athletes in the future who may be struggling.

Michelle

Michelle Bergstrand was 48 when we met. I interviewed her at her home. I had never met Michelle before and we had been introduced for the sole purpose of this book.

Another common fear surrounding psychoanalysts is that within a few seconds of meeting you, "they" will have worked you out. Again, a myth I wish to dispel. How can anyone know a person's entire modus operandi within a few seconds of meeting? Our minds and internal worlds are much more complex than this. However, that being said, the first thing that Michelle did say to me once we settled for our interview was that she was going to sit on the floor as her "back is knackered". For the duration of her interview this meant that Michelle remained on the floor as I sat in an armchair. A constant reminder that Michelle was in pain. This first, throwaway comment made by Michelle did not tell me everything I needed to know about her, but it was important. Pain was a constant feature for Michelle and so too was her long-standing relationship to pain.

Background

Michelle was from an army family; her father was a warrant officer and her mother was described as an army wife. Michelle also had a sister. She told me that her upbringing was "cold" and "shitty" and that she was always moving around so she never felt able to settle and to be a part of a group. This pattern was repeated in schools where she would start to integrate with her peers and then her father would be reposted and they would be off again. Michelle's sister used to run and from the age of 12 Michelle started cross-country herself. She ran at county level and then moved to North Yorkshire to complete her degree in business studies and it was here that she found the moors. She felt at home there, the sense of isolation was familiar to her, much like the sense of isolation that she had felt all throughout her upbringing.

In a conversation with her mother, the mother asked if she was that bad a parent, and Michelle responded by saying that she wasn't a horrendous parent but the environment in which she and her sister were brought up in was "destructive". Michelle clarified, "destructive for me".

She described her mother as very loyal but cold, argumentative, and fiery. She explained how her mother grew up in Glasgow in a comfortable environment, but that she was the youngest of eight siblings. Her mother and father were married within nine months of knowing each other. Michelle believes that her father had always provided her mother with everything material that she ever needed and so being told no and tolerating others' needs or the need for compromise or negotiation is something that her mother never had to experience.

In a recent argument, shortly before Michelle's interview, her mother punched her in the face. It was at this point that Michelle enforced a boundary and stopped all contact with her. Michelle recalled that her upbringing and more recent times shared an environment characterised by a mother who was unable to manage her emotions and one who would direct her aggression towards Michelle. She described her father as a man who could be selfish with his emotions and his time and was never one to give or show praise. She told me how she was given no guidance in life. She explained that this is why she ended up in the North as she wanted to go to the university that was furthest away from her parents. Michelle also experienced her sister as a "bully", always feeling that she was just in her way.

During her time at university, 1988–92, Michelle injured her back when she fell running, and entered a mountain bike race instead. She won it and was sponsored within a week. The girl who came second went on to become an Olympian. Michelle ended up riding at elite level full time; however, her lack of confidence was always something that held her back. She competed at the Worlds in 1993 and was on the British Cyclo-Cross squad. There was a group of about four or six female cyclists who were earmarked for the 1996 Olympics in Atlanta but only two were accepted. In 1995, Michelle contracted one virus after another and she knew she wasn't going to be chosen to go to the Olympics. Her back injury was also causing her difficulties and so in 1996 she retired and joined the police. Michelle was uncertain what career she wished to pursue and even thought about joining the army as an officer once she had completed her degree. By this time, she had met her husband and so joining the police felt like a better fit. She then also returned to racing as a Master in 2000. She became elite again, won a number of Master's titles and European Master's titles on the track and in mountain biking. In 2008, Michelle was in a position where she was now divorced and had her two children, aged five and eight at the time. They had started to become interested in sport and dance and a conscious decision was made to put her children first; however, training has always been a mainstay in Michelle's life, dipping her toe into racing every now and then.

She told me that it was never the plan to be a cyclist; the only reason she raced on the first day that resulted in her winning and receiving sponsorship was because her then husband was an international mountain runner. Michelle couldn't keep up with him when running but when they hired mountain bikes suddenly she could. He did a bit of mountain bike racing and encouraged Michelle to try herself and this was how it all started. Michelle told me that the early 1990s was an incredible time for mountain biking especially for the elites, and looking back she doubted that this was ever something that would be repeated. It was the inception of racing to the UK and she told me that some "legends" were born around this time. Even though Michelle received sponsorship with Orange, she did not have the support that athletes get nowadays and she had to find her own way.

Relationship templates: isolation and bullying

Michelle's early experiences and family environment had exposed her to a relationship template where others are either cold and unavailable or they bully you. The theory of object relations (how we relate to others and ourselves) suggests that these templates are laid down at an early age, become internalised and are then repeated. I've drawn a small diagram just to try to show this more simply.

The individual consciously desires something different, something more emotionally satisfying but unconsciously they are drawn to what they have always known, even if it may look slightly different on the surface. It feels familiar, comfortable and there is a wish that the disturbing dynamic can be mastered and controlled. In practice, we may all be able to relate this to victims of domestic abuse. Despite countless attempts at trying to support individuals to leave an abusive relationship, more often than not individuals go back. Michelle was not a stranger to abusive dynamics and her second marriage was to an abusive man who

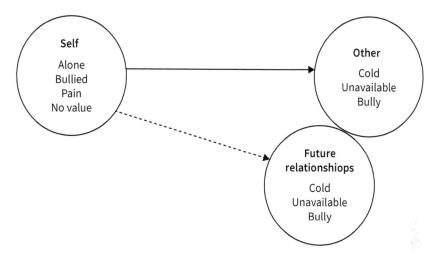

Figure 3 Diagram of relationships template

continued to harass her following the end of their relationship. Michelle took six months off work at this time and saw a counsellor.

If she was identifying with the template position of individuals being cold and unavailable, her experience was one of isolation and a sense of lack, as if something was missing for her. She described how she has always felt like the individual that was on the outside. During her first marriage, her husband was headhunted and they moved to Australia. Michelle took a career break for a year and it was the isolation that eventually led to her depression and a return to the UK. In retrospect, she was able to tell me that the isolation does not manifest itself from her external environment but instead it is something that lives within her from a continuous longing for a family dynamic that she has never had. We will come to explore Michelle's depression later in the chapter when we think about the impact of space.

She told me how the moorlands were "absolutely her", either running on her own or with a small group of select people. Michelle lives in an area where there are lots of running groups; however, she struggles to be a part of these as she doesn't always want to do what they do and instead she wishes to do what she wants. Just like her mother, Michelle struggles with compromise. She told me that she always has her own agenda and that she thinks this is "terrible" as it continues to maintain her isolation from bigger groups and holds others in the position of being unavailable. She told me about cycling groups that exist on Facebook but she struggles to turn up because it feels as if she is being dictated to; and this is something that she has always felt, rather than a sense of being listened to, understood and taken into consideration. Michelle explained that she grew up feeling very scared of doing anything wrong. There were lots of fights, screaming, shouting and arguing and so her coping mechanism was to stay quiet and to "toe the party line".

Masochism

Toeing the party line, as Michelle put it, was an effective way to cope in the environment she grew up in. However, the risk of toeing the party line for ever more is that an individual's own position is not expressed, respected or valued. With this comes not only an entire lack of value in one's self but also annoyance and frustration at being silenced. The frustration should of course be directed at the object (person) that is dictating, telling you what to do and not listening. Over time, if this maintains itself, lack of confidence, low self-esteem, and anger easily develop. If anger is not directed externally at the person that is making you angry for fear of what may result from this, it is likely to then be turned inwards and can express itself in the form of masochism. Anger does not just disappear; it needs to be thought about, processed and/or discharged.

Earlier, Michelle told me that it had always been her lack of confidence that had held her back from achieving more in her sport. Paradoxically, as we will now come to explore, it is likely that the same mechanism that has caused her lack of confidence has also caused the masochism that feeds her training and ability to compete. As already mentioned in my introduction, it is likely that a lot of athletes are skewed to the right with regard to masochism, given how, in order to succeed in sport, pushing through a pain threshold during training and competition is familiar territory for so many a sportsperson. For those with lower pain thresholds or those who do not experience any pleasure from pushing through the pain barrier, it is likely that they would give up earlier. They would not likely achieve as much as those with higher tolerance levels and/or an unconscious degree of aggression that can be discharged in this way.

Now, just to clarify what I mean by masochism. During the interview, when I introduced the term to Michelle for the first time, she reminded me that the popular association to masochism for most people is that of "people beating themselves up and tying themselves up in chains!". Masochism is something I am familiar with in my day-to-day work, so my associations are not as popularised or indeed negative, because we all have masochistic parts within us. There is a whole spectrum of masochism, which ranges from the extreme whereby some people do derive pleasure or relief from causing pain to themselves. Here we may think of those that self-harm or self-injure. Some very well-known athletes have spoken about engaging in self-harm. This has included the likes of Victoria Pendleton and Dame Kelly Holmes. I do not, however, know either of their stories or developmental backgrounds, so I'm unable to comment on the causation of their self-harm. At the other end of the spectrum we could observe someone who is constantly placing themselves in situations that result in failure, in other words, self-sabotage, is someone who is engaging in masochism. This experience for many, though, is not experienced as consciously pleasurable; it is instead responding to an unconscious need. Think again of our domestic violence victim. I'm sure not many would report experiencing conscious pleasure when they are being physically abused. Masochism is therefore, in psychoanalysis, seen as a defence against aggression. It is a response to aggression where if the individual does not feel able to express this externally by displaying their anger or it feels too dangerous for them to display their anger, they may respond by turning this anger inwards and causing pain to themselves—and this does not always mean physical pain. Where the definition gets more challenging is the association with how pleasure is derived from this intentional cause of pain to the self. Again, it is not always a typical excitable pleasure that is experienced, and with Michelle we are able to explore how sometimes the pleasure derived from pain can be more subtle.

During the interview, Michelle told me that she had retired from cycling on a number of occasions across the years. She then confirmed that she had never really retired; the Zwift equipment in her kitchen (bike, turbo trainer, and app for training with the cycling community) and the very fact that Michelle arrived late to our interview due to being out on a training ride were testament to this. She told me that even now her week revolved around training. Michelle had negotiated to work part-time to manage family commitments and this also allows her to get out on her bike in the morning. The police also have a desire to back sport and exercise given the positive effects on mental health. She told me that the thought of going to work without being able to get out on her bike "fuddles" her head. When I asked Michelle how she would feel if she couldn't train she told me she would be "panic stricken". We explored what this was about and, consciously, it appeared to be related to the fear of weight gain and decline in performance. However, as we spoke more, we realised that Michelle was not a "big mile muncher" but that she liked to "ride hard". For Michelle there was something about the intensity of her training and how in her head it was never enough, but that she could allow herself to stop if she had pushed hard and felt fatigue in her body. She measured fatigue by reaching the point where she is breathing hard, her legs are hurting, and she thinks she wants to stop but knows that she can't. More recently, she was trying to stop during her training rides as she had spent her life looking down at the floor never knowing what is going on around her. Now, when she stops to climb over gates, she stops and looks and maybe even takes a photograph. Michelle laughed and told me that the trouble was, it is the same photograph on the same training route each week.

Michelle had helpfully identified that what motivated and continued to motivate her was a need to reach a high intensity that resulted in a discharge of energy that pushed her to the point of hurting. If this was not a part of her daily training schedule she was "panic stricken". I spent almost three hours with Michelle on the day of her interview. In the final ten minutes I asked her if she would ever let herself stop and she stated:

> No, I need that physical outlet. I suppose it's almost like a case of some people's release of angst through self-harm … That's where it crosses over with masochism … Aaah I've got there in the end! You see, this morning I didn't want to get out of bed but I got up, rode and felt like crap but I felt euphoric when I'd done it. Ticked that box, felt good.

For Michelle, her sport and training had become a way of managing her anger related to her developmental experiences. However, as this could not be expressed outwardly, she was expressing this through sport. She is able to identify that she feels crap when she wakes in the morning: she has not yet been able to express her anger externally and so instead she discharges her anger in her sport and feels euphoric afterwards. Sadly, the aggression directed at herself has resulted in physical damage, pain, and a refusal to stop when injured. This is, however, what motivates Michelle and has allowed her to achieve everything that she has done in her sport. Her relationship to pain is long-standing and complex.

At the age of ten, when purchasing a pair of trainers, Michelle recalls not being able to bend down to do the laces up. It was from this point onwards that she experienced pain in her back. She has two prolapsed discs in her spine and a diagnosis of stenosis. Stenosis is the narrowing of the spinal channel where eventually the nerves and the spinal cord compress resulting in severe pain, weakness and/or numbness. Michelle also experiences pain and weakness in her right leg and generates 30% less power than in her left leg. She explained that the pain is worse if she is standing or leant backwards and so when she is bent forwards she experiences some relief. She dreads cooking as her leg will often go dead and she has to bring a stool up to the bench to allow her to sit down.

Despite training daily, Michelle's pain impacts upon her work. She would not be able to go on foot patrol as she would be sitting on a wall. If she was given a rucksack and was leaning forward, she told me, things are not as bad. On the Sunday before we met, Michelle had been on a six-mile run. The first 20 minutes were agony but as long as she can run up a big hill the pain eases as she is able to lean forwards. After 20 minutes, she told me, she had forgotten about the pain. I asked if Michelle ever stopped. Quickly, she told me, "No, I refuse to." I asked if Michelle stopped to allow for recovery if she was ever injured. This is a point where she really struggles. In the past she has injured her Achilles tendon and she was unable to run for around eight weeks. Despite this, she kept trying. Admittedly, Michelle told me that if it was someone she was coaching it would be an entirely different story.

Michelle's inability to stop training when injured is consistent with the thinking that her sport provides her with a way of discharging energy or anger in a masochistic way. Without it, she struggles. I wanted to explore if Michelle did derive any conscious pleasure from the pain she experienced. She told me that this was difficult to answer as she was always in pain, it really was her template way of being. She then confirmed that she did get pleasure out of the pain. When it came to her bodily pain, such as in her back injury, she told me that she thought she got pleasure out of beating it and getting through it. I reflected that beating it was not making the pain go away, though. Michelle agreed. On the morning of the interview, she had also walked her dog, and at the corner before her house she experienced "horrendous back pain". She thought to herself that she could stop and stretch but she chose not to and consciously thought, I'm going to keep going. It appeared that Michelle was continuing to repeat her historical experience of pain not only in her sport but also in her everyday activities. Freud[1] believes that we find comfort in the familiar and furthermore repeat our historical experiences in a hope that over time we may come to master the beast. For Michelle, I wondered if perhaps her refusal to stop when she experiences pain was about her unconscious hopes to master and overcome her internal pain.

Eating/weight gain

Another reason that Michelle gave for not being able to stop training was the fear of weight gain. When she was younger she experienced eating difficulties. She consciously felt that this was about control as she felt she had so little in her family environment. Initially she opted to go vegetarian. This made her dad "furious"; however, her mother said to "just leave it". Michelle started to lose weight and got down to 6 stone 8 pounds, measuring 5 foot 3 inches in height. Her friend did it too. The following year in cross-country she did really badly whereas her friend went from 97th position to 4th in the British Nationals and got GB team selection. Michelle remained vegetarian for 14 years. When training in a squad environment, Michelle would become panicked

---

[1] Freud, S. (1914g). "Remembering, Repeating and Working-through (Further Recommendations on the Technique of Psycho-Analysis, II)". *S. E., 12*. London: Hogarth.

as she felt that she had to justify if she did not want dessert or butter. She never made herself sick but just restricted her food intake. Between the ages of 16 and 19 she did not menstruate for a couple of years, suggesting that her fat percentage was too low for a female adult.

Michelle's eating restriction or control is not mutually exclusive to her masochism. Masochism can be displayed in many different symptoms. Self-harm is one, excessive exercising despite injury and pain is another, and eating disorders is yet another. It is a way of turning anger inwards again at your own body. Consciously, Michelle thought it was about control. However, what is also interesting is her father's response to Michelle becoming vegetarian. It made him "furious". Her father, the typically absent parent was now angry and Michelle had found a way to make this happen. One theory of eating disorders is that the anorectic is actually using her own body unconsciously to control and attack her internalised parents as she feels unable to attack them externally.[2] This internalised mother refers to the process that occurs during development where we internalise parts of our mother and our father and they become parts of who we are. In popular parlance you may relate to the saying: "We all become our mother one day".

Working in the police

Michelle's career choice at face value was not a surprise to me and I wonder if you as a reader are also not surprised. It was now my turn to express my own naïve popular understanding of the role of a police officer. Given that much of our discussions were around masochism and aggression, I wrongly assumed that Michelle's career choice of working in the police must have been about offering her a socially acceptable way to express her aggression towards individuals that may be deemed as "abusers" or "bullies" in society. It was Michelle's turn to educate me and here she told me that she worked in collision investigation. Her work involved dealing with fatalities and with road safety. She is exposed to photos of catastrophic injuries on a daily basis

---

[2] Lawrence, M. (2001). Loving them to death: The anorexic and her objects. *International Journal of Psychoanalysis, 82*: 43–55.

but this does not seem to faze her now. She has been working in the police for the past 23 years and in collision investigation for the past five years. Dealing with the aftermath of an accident is something that she does very well. While working as an ordinary officer, she struggled to manage dealing with assaults and domestic disputes. She is not an officer who takes pleasure in arresting people and, instead, she likes to go in and try to fix or make things better. I was surprised by this comment as again, naïvely, I shared the thought that after a fatal collision there wasn't much left to fix.

Michelle educated me that you can't fix the person who has died but you can "soften the blow" and try to bring some justice or closure to the family involved. She feels privileged to do her job because she is a part of something that has just changed someone's world and it is possible she can make life just that bit easier at that time. She could be there to listen. This was something that she had never had. She told me that it can happen to any of us. We drive from A to B, get distracted, hit someone, and you're an offender. Michelle is mindful that she wishes to make the whole process as "painless as possible for both sides". The language that Michelle was using did not need a psychologist to interpret why she was working in the area she was. It was clear to me that Michelle's relationship to pain was so intrinsic to what motivated and drove her that an externalisation of her own wish and desire to reduce the pain in her own life meant she was instead attempting to minimise the pain associated to one of the most horrific things that can happen to anyone in their lives. This externalisation of one's own wishes can happen in many professions. Michelle is not alone. The caring profession is renowned for being populated largely by those individuals who unconsciously wish and desire care for themselves but struggle to receive it. A sweeping generalisation, but not uncommon.

When does something become unhealthy?

Earlier on you may recall that I asked Michelle how she would feel if she didn't train. She told me that she would feel "panic stricken". I'm often asked as a psychologist working with athletes and coaches, how do you know when something has tipped over into something more concerning?

For me, there are two fundamental things that have to be present that may indicate it is the right time to start thinking about working with a therapist. It is a given that clinical symptoms are present, but as we explore in other chapters, this in itself does not always equate to "time to get help". The big distinction for me is that first, the symptoms themselves or the consequences of the symptoms have become distressing to the individual. They are no longer functional.

For Michelle, for so long, her training and competing were functional to her. They offered her a socially acceptable way of managing and coping with her anger and aggression and lack of emotional support. Michelle was engaging in her sport because it was functional and it worked. It helped her cope. We all possess coping strategies: some are healthier than others but if they are working for the individual it is not my job as a psychologist or psychotherapist to come in with a bulldozer and break down these defences. To play devil's advocate, one may actually suggest that engaging in excessive exercise is a lesser evil than engaging in excessive drug use. It's just a different poison.

As the American Psychiatric Association's *Diagnostic and Statistical Manual of Mental Disorders* states, in order for a diagnosis to be present, symptoms must cause "clinically significant distress or impairment in social, occupational, or other important areas of functioning".

Second, a key indicator for me that sport may be being used defensively to manage something unconscious or troubling, is when athletes report, just like Michelle, that they cannot stop training and they fear what may happen if they stop. Typically, if sport is being used to fill a gap, to distract or to avoid something unconscious, it is likely that when the person stops engaging in sport, they find space in their lives and in their mind. Training at a high-performance level ensures that your weekly timetable is full. Very effective at offering distraction or switching the mind off if you do not wish to explore something troubling. Once this space is freed up, it is then likely that the contents of your mind which you have been trying to avoid start to surface.

Michelle struggles with space. She told me that when she has an hour, she has to fill it. Her experience, though, is that her time is not always used constructively and she can postulate and think about what needs to get done. When she followed her first husband to Australia, she was half a mile from the Indian Ocean, it was sunny every day, and she had made friends. The physical distance and space, however, connected her with the fear that she was so far away from her family and that she felt isolated. This time her isolation was not a comfortable feeling but instead resulted in a "blackness" and Michelle became depressed.

In recent months, after the physical altercation with her mother, Michelle has been able to realise that she was missing her family and a relationship that had never been there. It had always been a lack. Winnicott[3] talks about the importance of containment or a sense of holding. This is not a physical holding that is being referred to but an emotional sense of being held in someone's mind and the other being able to tolerate and manage your emotional needs with you. This was lacking for Michelle and it is understandable that space and relationships have always presented a challenge to her. It was likely that Michelle's sport afforded her the opportunity to fill that space and to engage in an environment where she could function on her own on a bike, on a track, or on a mountain. If that wasn't present, Michelle may have had to connect to this lack and the associated emotional pain rather than the physical pain created by her sport.

The other presenting difficulty for Michelle was one of value. Throughout the interview she had alluded to how she has always struggled with her confidence and how she feared failure. Another fallout of experiencing a lack in the family environment is how the child is not noticed and struggles to internalise a sense of value. During my visit, Michelle told me how she enjoyed drawing and sometimes if she is able to find space she will, on rare occasions, take the opportunity to draw. The week before I arrived, she had done a pencil drawing of her great aunt, who was an actress in *Fawlty Towers*. I asked if I could see the work and she showed me. It was a beautiful piece of artwork and I verbalised this. Michelle was unable to hear it and stated, "No, I don't think it's that good at all. No, it's not." For someone who is unable to see value in themselves, Michelle's masochism, her behaviours and choices should now make more sense. To hurt oneself repeatedly

---

[3] Winnicott, D. W. (1960). The theory of the parent-child relationship. *International Journal of Psychoanalysis, 41*: 585–595.

through behaviour and to engage in relationships that are abusive, all communicates how someone is maintaining a belief that they are not worth more.

For Michelle, her battle continues and she tells me how she will always be "chasing the dragon". She has, however, more recently been able to introduce boundaries into her relationships and this is starting to communicate some respect for herself. I hope that in time Michelle can start to see the value she possesses, not as a cyclist, but as an individual in her own right.

Summary

Masochism may be seen as a defence against aggression. If the individual does not feel able or it feels too dangerous to express this externally then they may respond by turning aggression inwards and causing pain to themselves—this does not always mean physical pain.

Michelle's story has allowed us to explore how developmental experiences, internalised template ways of being and relating to oneself, to others and to chosen environments can maintain this. Michelle needed a vehicle to discharge her aggression in a socially acceptable way and she found cycling. The definition of masochism can challenge, given the association with how pleasure is derived from this intentional cause of pain to the self. Michelle's story allows us to understand that masochism is often unconscious and nuanced and that she does not experience conscious pleasure in pain itself but pleasure in getting through the pain and beating it. In this way, Michelle feels that she has mastery over managing her external pain. However, Michelle remains aware that her cycling and mastery over this external pain fill an internal void. A void that has been created by a lack of feeling held in someone's mind or being cared for in a more tender way. When training is lost and space is felt, this void is overwhelming and historically Michelle has experienced periods of depression.

Sportspeople are familiar with pain. In order to be great and to excel at what they do, it is inherent that the individual will have to push through the pain barrier and not give up easily. This in itself is not masochism. However, it is important that the athlete remains aware of when pushing through the pain barrier and living in the far right end of the normal distribution (being skewed to the right) may be tipping over into something unhealthy. I suggest that there are two criteria to consider:

1. Are the behaviours and/or symptoms causing significant distress or impairment in social, occupational, or other important areas of functioning?
2. Is there an inability to stop training/engaging with the chosen sport and an overwhelming fear associated to the thought of stopping?

If both criteria are satisfied, it is possible that the individual would benefit from exploring their relationship to sport and exercise in a therapeutic environment.

CHAPTER 4

Obsessionality

In order to become a high-performance athlete, there is the understanding and expectation that one will be devoted to a chosen sport. For those who take their sport seriously, this includes strict adherence to one's training programme. This then becomes part of a wider lifestyle choice ... I need to be up at 6 am to be in the gym, I'll go to bed at 9.30 pm to ensure I get at least eight hours' sleep. I need to support two training sessions per day, therefore I need to eat 4,000 calories and drink at least 8 litres of fluid. I have a competition on Saturday, so I will taper my training in the week leading up to this and not have sex ...

Suddenly, the life of a high-performance athlete becomes a pervasive lifestyle choice that not only impacts upon food, drink, alcohol, and drug consumption, but also impacts upon sleep, work, holidays, sex, social and familial relationships, and activity choices outside sport. The individual must be selfish. Selfishness has become a pejorative term and I wish to explore that here. To be selfish, the *Oxford English Dictionary* defines as to be "concerned chiefly with one's own profit or pleasure at the expense of consideration for others". Is there anything wrong with this? Is this still OK? What if one's partner is in full support of one's goals, does that make it OK? And what if by acting selfishly one can achieve sporting greatness that no other person has ever achieved? These are all questions where there are no clear answers. They are, however, questions that every high-performance athlete is confronted with. Some may argue that the most focused do not have a relationship with these questions. I would argue that they do, be it consciously or unconsciously, by the very behaviour they are engaging in. These questions are ever present, even if they are buried beyond conscious awareness.

For the sake of this chapter, I would prefer to use the term *egocentric* to refer to athlete behaviour. In Freud's theory of personality structure,[4] he suggests the three parts are the id, ego, and superego. In very basic terms, the id responds to the innate drives within all of us (food, sex, pleasure). The superego is our moral compass; it keeps our id in check, ensuring that we do not allow our id to run on full throttle at all times. The ego is the thinking part of the self which mediates between the id and the superego. To be egocentric, one is focused on oneself: it is an inward-looking position to the exclusion of consideration of others. Piaget sees this as a necessary, healthy developmental stage that is moved through by all children. The outcome is that children may then look outside themselves and think about the thoughts, feelings, and behaviours of others and realise that they may differ from their own. They develop what is called a theory of mind. Perhaps we can say by the very nature of their goals, our high-performance athletes are all egocentric in nature, that is, they are inwardly focused despite having a developed theory of mind and while they consciously know the impact of their behaviour on others.

So, when does behaviour become obsessive? Or is all sporting behaviour obsessive in nature? If high-performance athletes aren't obsessive and egocentric then perhaps they just wouldn't be as successful as they are. So, what's the problem with being obsessive? For many, maybe it isn't a problem. Maybe it's a good thing that supports them in achieving their goals. How would problematic obsessiveness be measured anyway? I may not have a partner and I may have missed my sister's wedding this year but I won gold at Rio. Is this problematic or is this worth it? Perhaps it becomes one's own measure of weighing up the benefits against the cost of the sacrifices and the consequences that follow as a result. Sacrifice is key

---

[4] Freud, S. (1923b). *The Ego and the Id. S. E., 19.* London: Hogarth.

to this. With obsessionality and egocentrism come exclusion, isolation, and sacrifice. Yet, what if you can't switch it off and obsessionality is functional in the sporting arena but it is dysfunctional in one's everyday life? Obsessively counting out reps in the gym is one thing, but obsessively counting out flicks of a light switch is another.

Jonny Wilkinson, one time England rugby player, has spoken openly about his own challenges with obsessionality and perfectionism, in the media and in a number of books. At the peak of his career, he was known for obsessively practising kicking and would not leave practice sessions until he had achieved six successful kicks (according to the media). During competition, this meant he pretty much nailed it every time. Off the pitch, and on the pitch sometimes, Jonny's obsessionality and strive for perfectionism was much more challenging, again according to the media, preventing enjoyment across all areas of his life. If you recall from my thoughts earlier in the masochism chapter, about when do we know that we are hitting a clinical threshold, it appears possible that Jonny had hit that criterion as his behaviour was causing significant distress or impairment in his social, occupational, and/or everyday functioning. The degree to which his obsessionality was skewed to the right may have tipped over into something clinical, despite it being incredibly helpful to his sporting achievements. A position of huge vulnerability for the athlete. Do they dare meet with a psychologist to work on their mental health issues? If they do, does this mean that the level of obsessionality which helps them perform and achieve greatness will be lost but they will be able to function in everyday life? This can cause huge internal conflict and is one reason why many athletes avoid the clinical psychologist.

What drives someone to become obsessed, to sacrifice so much? A gold medal? A title? Why is a piece of metal and a few words attached to one's name so intently focused on, through tunnel vision, to the exclusion of everything else in one's life? Eddie Hall, World's Strongest Man in 2017, is famously known for saying that he was going to be the next World's Strongest Man or he would die trying. This is a man who is prepared to make the biggest sacrifice of all for his chosen sporting goal: his life. Or was he really? Was this just offered up as a communication of how dedicated this man was to reach his goals? I knew there was one man who would be happy and able to talk to me about the obsessive nature of training and what drives someone to dedicate themselves to their sport. This man was Luke Stoltman.

Luke

I first met Luke in a gym in Newcastle. I was still rowing recreationally at the time and Luke was working away from home. We were both engaging in our regular weekly routine of squatting in the squat rack when we got talking. At the time of interview in 2018, Luke was five-times Scotland's strongest man, the first Scot to compete in World's Strongest Man for approximately 15 years and the only Scotsman to have competed three years in a row. He had ranked fourth in Britain's Strongest Man and 12th at the World's two years in a row, in 2016 and 2017.

Luke lives in the Highlands of Scotland, in Inverness. He has always lived there and feels an absolute sense of pride about his country and his home town. He comes from a big family, being the eldest of five siblings and many cousins. He was expelled from school at the age of 15 for publishing a website that made up rumours about his school teachers. Apparently, one in particularly referred to a certain teacher "shagging a donkey". He told me that he was mischievous and took the blame for a group of four of his friends that had also been involved in the prank. He explained that his mother wasn't really that bothered and perhaps just knew that school wasn't for him. Despite this, she did fight the case for Luke to sit his exams but by this time he did not care. He believes that his mother would have liked for him to have done better academically and to maybe have gone to university, but this was not something that Luke achieved.

Luke as the eldest was followed by two sisters and two brothers. He told me that he used to lead by example. His youngest brother, Tom, who has a diagnosis of Asperger's syndrome, now also competes on the strongman circuit. Their mother had always been their biggest fan until she passed away to cancer in 2016. She used to make T-shirts for all of the strongman competitions and she could be heard shouting support from the crowd. Luke has kept every T-shirt that his mother had ever made. He used to laugh watching the videos of competitions. He could hear his mother shouting for his brother Tom and he would jest with her that Tom was now the favourite son. Luke told me that as long as both he and his brother came away healthy at the end of it all, she was happy.

Growing up, Luke's father worked away on the oil rigs and the family environment was a traditional one. His mother stayed home and looked after the five children while Luke's father provided for them financially. He described how his mother was everything to him, the good, the bad, and the ugly, and how his father would come back from working away and would get all the pleasurable aspects of being a parent.

The other male figure in Luke's life therefore became his grandfather. He lived next door and I was told that this was a man that you just respected. Opa, as affectionately named by the family, was from Poland. He had made his way to Inverness after being given asylum as a Polish prisoner of war. Luke had an awareness of the hardships that his grandfather must have faced and how he came out the other side and was a well-known, respected man in the local community. Luke admired his grandfather. He worked on the land digging peats for the fire. Luke recalls his father telling him about how Opa would go out in the freezing cold snow and work all day chopping peats and loading them in the back of the Land Rover. Today, society is "too soft" he told me. Opa was a "hardy bastard" with a strong work ethic.

Despite not respecting any of his teachers, Luke respected Opa. Two to three generations ago "you just had to work" and Luke told me that this is what Opa did "to just keep going". He was known for employing local youths and men who were alcoholics or struggling, and he would take them up into the hills to detox a bit, hold onto the money they had earned, and then give this to their wives at the end of the week so they didn't spend it.

It frightened Luke to think of what his grandfather had had to endure, to have to leave his home country and to learn of how his sister, brother, and parents had died, that they had been shot dead in his absence. It was a reality that Opa lost a lot of his family back home in Poland as a consequence of the war. Luke's respect for Opa related to how he had endured such adversity and had survived and still achieved in the way that he did.

Luke's relationship to mental health and addiction was therefore quite stern. He told me how he was frustrated with the amount of people talking openly about their struggles with depression and addiction.

He was of the opinion that his generation has been given too much. When he looks at what his grandfather had to endure and how he still came out the other side, he doesn't understand why others can't too. Later in the interview, I asked Luke if he felt that his grandfather was traumatised by his experiences and he responded by saying, "Maybe, yeah, I mean he did like to drink." He told me that he would often sit quietly in his garden. He liked to be by himself, in a special spot that used to be called "Opa's garden".

What is a strongman?

No one in Luke's family went to the gym, but Luke knew he wanted to lift big weights; it seemed like a normal thing for a man to do. At the start of his training, Luke confessed it was more about vanity; at this stage he was more interested in the bodybuilding scene. He liked the feedback from others that he was receiving, being told how big he was getting and how strong he was. It was not until a friend encouraged him to enter Scotland's Strongest Man that he had even considered competing in strongman events. Preparing for his first competition, Luke was scared of failing. He recalls how he got drunk the night before and almost convinced himself not to go. For some reason, though, he turned up, slightly tipsy, and won it. He thought he must be onto something if he could do that with minimal training. That was that, he had caught the bug and wanted to beat everyone. When Luke was younger, he recalled not liking getting beaten at running races but he did not know where this mentality had come from. He told me that he would get a "well done" from his mum and dad regardless of whether he won. His father was never really sporty, he played a bit of rugby but was mainly interested in shooting and fishing. Regardless, second place to him was fine but it was "first place loser".

Luke thought for some time and struggled to think where his mentality had come from and what was motivating him. He wasn't sure. He told me that he didn't feel he needed to be something, but, maybe, coming from a bigger family meant it was nice that there was something that could be celebrated about his achievements. He enjoys playing to the crowds at competitions and, since the death of his mother, he often thinks about her, and this drives him on in the hope that he is doing her justice.

There was a theme that was starting to establish itself in Luke's family history and this was one of respected family members being lost, almost like fallen soldiers in the background. For Luke, masculinity and the role of a strong man was that of someone who was able to lift big weights but also to provide for the family financially, to protect them, and to keep them safe. His own traditional upbringing meant that he wanted to be financially stable enough to look after his own wife and to say to her that she doesn't have to work unless she wants to.

Training regime

Luke works offshore as a dimensional surveyor, so his work pattern means he is typically offshore for two weeks and then onshore at home for two weeks. He described how he has to optimise this window and train heavy when at home. Gym equipment and weights are available offshore but being on a floating barge means that the ground is always moving and sometimes, if the weather is too rough, the gym is closed for health and safety reasons.

He typically arrives home on a Friday night and has a big "scoff" where he consumes a large amount of carbohydrates to get his energy levels high for Saturday. During Saturday daytime, he will work on conditioning and maybe do some work on events (such as sandbag carries or yoke walks). Conditioning can be typically 30 minutes' high-intensity cardio. On Saturday evening he does a heavy dead lift or squat session. Sunday will be the same again and this will be repeated every day whilst at home.

Luke confirmed that training twice a day was the norm and he tries to maintain this when he is offshore as well. Offshore, he wakes at 4.30 am and trains on the upright bike for half an hour and then does some core work. Following his shift on a night-time he will go to the gym. However, the equipment he has access to is limited. He views his time onshore as intense and heavy and offshore as more rest and recovery with higher rep lighter weights.

Diet is also more challenging while Luke is away offshore. When at home, he eats six-plus meals a day, whereas when he is offshore, he is given three meals a day that are not bad, but are not ideal for what he is trying to achieve. Luke does not have access to a nutritionist but he does try to keep up to date with research and observe what the other strongmen competitors do.

He estimated that he probably consumes around 5,000+ calories a day which typically consists of the main food groups: carbs, protein, and vegetables. He will eat a lot of sweet potato, oats, chicken, steak, vegetables, and rice. Luke supplements his diet with protein shakes but these are just used as an additive to his diet if he requires a quick intake before a workout. He also uses branch chain amino acids during a workout. He only sleeps for five or six hours at night and always wakes early. He would like to sleep more, but if he is home, he feels that he is missing things if asleep. He wakes at 6 am, his wife goes to work, and he will then train and have a lie-down afterwards. He can typically have a couple of naps during the day as long as he is training and eating right. He does not weigh himself but goes on how he looks in the mirror. His competition weight is 155 kg and he knows when he is on target as he looks lean. Luke does allow himself treats in the form of the "odd takeaway" but he told me this typically happened when he was being lazy and he hadn't prepared things. Luke spoke about not really wanting to seek the advice of a nutritionist as he felt he would struggle with them being in a position of authority, just like his teachers used to be. He told me that they didn't know him or his body and how it reacts to different things, so he would always be apprehensive.

Another area—the elephant in the room with a 155 kg man sat in front of me—was that of performance-enhancing drugs. Strongman competitions are categorised either as natural strongman or strongman, where recreational drugs alone are tested for, so it is accepted that performance-enhancing drugs are used. This is similar for powerlifting; there are natural powerlifting competitions and powerlifting competitions. Despite this, it appeared to be a topic that was still considered taboo, and Luke believes this is not helping matters, as people remain uneducated and as a consequence are making misinformed decisions. He also spoke of his frustrations about how steroids hold negative associations in society and can be spoken about incorrectly in the media, being blamed for causing early deaths in gym goers. Performance-enhancing drugs are wide-ranging and can include the use of steroids, growth hormone, peptides, designer steroids, pro hormones, and there is also the use of blood transfusions and plasma drips. With such a plethora of performance-enhancement options that were allowed, but considered taboo, I wondered if this was one area where a cultural change needed to happen.

My discussions with Luke reminded me of the recent shift in management of drugs at music festivals. There is now an awareness that some people are going to take drugs regardless of whether you attempt to stop them or not. Therefore, one response to this has been to test the contents of drugs to ensure that if people are going to take them, what they are taking is not mixed with anything toxic. I wondered if perhaps something could be learnt from this and, given that performance-enhancing drugs are accepted in some sports, perhaps education surrounding their use and testing of products purchased online would be a responsible public health decision. Turning to my earlier chapter where I interviewed Mark Enright, I wonder if some education regarding supplements, laxatives, diuretics, and the use of other drugs with jockeys would have prevented Mark from consuming the dangerous amount of Lasix that he did.

Addiction and habit formation

It is important to share Luke's regime, not just his exercise, but his diet, sleep, and supplementation programme. Reading the details of his plan and how his day establishes itself around his training needs will elicit a slightly different reaction in all of us. We all have a subjective measure of what may sound impressive, excessive, or just "plain mad". I wanted to know if Luke thought that he was obsessed.

His response, instead, focused more around addiction. He felt more comfortable with this as a term to describe what he was doing. He agreed that there is a form of addiction that exists in sport and that he is addicted to a certain lifestyle, what he is putting in his body, and his work ethic. He told me that if he doesn't go to the gym for five days he is "panicking"; he then corrected himself and said, "Not panicking but I'm getting agitated." He described it as a withdrawal where he goes cold turkey and needs to train to top up his endorphins and the buzz that he gets from training. When he has a good gym session, he told me that he is buzzing; he described this as a high and how he was addicted to this feeling. He said with the gym, as long as you work hard, you can yield this feeling every time. If he and his wife, Kushi, were to go on holiday, Luke would not get his "fix" and this is why he feels he cannot go away.

Luke was actually onto something. His description of feeling a buzz after exercising was entirely accurate. Here's the science bit … Dopamine is a neurotransmitter that is associated with feelings of pleasure and satisfaction. It can be released by a number of behaviours inclusive of eating, sex, exercise, and drug addiction. Once felt, the pleasurable feeling can become sought after and behaviours are repeated to lead to the further release of more dopamine. Or, in Luke's words, to get his "fix".

The biology behind drug use and exercise is actually located in the same neurotransmitter system. Historically, dopamine's involvement in drug reinforcement was clear (i.e. I take drugs, I derive pleasure from this, therefore, behaviourally, this positive reinforcement means I want to take more). However, its role in drug addiction was less clear. More recently, in a paper by Johanshahi, Obeso, Rothwell, and Obeso,[5] they identify three pathways that implicate the basal ganglia and a wide range of cortical areas in habit formation and addiction. The basal ganglia are basically a group of structures in our brain that are associated with a variety of functions including control of voluntary action and habit formation. Johanshahi et al. explain how habit formation or addiction is just the acquisition of behaviours that are rewarding.

Initially, this is a behaviour that is thought about or cognitively derived: "I think I'm going to go to the gym," or "I think I'm going to take some drugs," but eventually, due to the effect of dopamine in the brain, it changes the action from one that is located in the limbic circuit and is cognitively derived, to an associative circuit that is emotionally derived, to a motor circuit that is automatic or habitual. In this way, exercise can be habit forming or addictive, just like drugs. Once the behaviour reaches the motor circuit, it becomes habitual and less rewarding and therefore more is required to get one's "fix", just as in drug addiction. In the same paper, Johanshahi et al. also explore the suggestion that obsessive-compulsive disorder (OCD) can be associated

---

[5] Johanshahi, M., Obeso, I., Rothwell, J. C., & Obeso, J. A. (2015). A fronto-striato-subthalamic-pallidal network for goal-directed and habitual inhibition. *Nature Reviews Neuroscience*, 16(12): 719–732.

with an imbalance of goal-directed behaviour versus habitual action localised again to the pathways in the basal ganglia. OCD is characterised by compulsions to engage in repetitive actions that could just be understood as the brain being unable to inhibit habitual action.

We therefore have a scientific basis that potentially supports how vulnerable our athletes are at the point of injury or retirement or even just at off-season. The degree of exercise that they have been engaging in has likely impacted upon the management of dopamine in their brain and greater levels of dopamine are required to yield pleasurable feedback or satisfaction.

It should therefore come as no surprise to us now, knowing this, that former athletes struggle with depression, alcoholism, and addiction if they are not able to train anymore or they are unable to engage in behaviours that yield similar pleasure, given their addiction. Potentially, exercise has no longer become a cognitive choice for them; it has become habitual and is needed to offset any low mood or depression. Furthermore, it is also important to acknowledge how vulnerable this may mean current athletes are to experiencing depression and engaging in alcohol and drug use during times of low season. We would expect that cricketers are particularly vulnerable at this time given the intense nature of their sport during the summer months compared to the winter months. We would expect that during low season, athletes may be seeking their "fix" in other ways if they are not able to train as much as they normally do, and the risk of not doing this may result in low mood or depression. In my next chapter, on focus, I will be exploring the impact of seasonal training and competition with cricketer Graeme Fowler and the seasonal ebb and flow to his depression.

We do, of course, have to be careful. I do not wish to be responsible for any incorrect sensationalist headlines regarding how "sport is bad for you" or "beware the addictive consequences of sport". Just as with alcohol and drugs, not everyone that decides to drink or take drugs on occasion presents with an addiction problem. It therefore follows that not everybody who engages in exercise and sport is going to present with an addiction problem or a depressive illness if they stop training. There are many individual, social, and cultural factors that contribute to addictions. They are a complex area of mental health and, just with sport, as this book is exploring, the factors that surround our high-performance athletes and what drives them and their potential vulnerability to developing mental health problems are also complex and multifaceted.

I had to ask, though, was Luke telling me that he never goes on holiday because he doesn't want to have to stop going to the gym for a period of time? Luke explained that if he takes two weeks off, he worries that it's two weeks away eating, drinking, and relaxing, and he has lost two weeks of training. This is especially so if it is during competition season but less so if it's off season. For the past couple of years, competition season has run from January to October and so only November and December are left to prepare for the next season. He told me he didn't want to go away anyway. Working offshore also means that Luke enjoys being at home when he gets the opportunity to do so. The compromise is that his wife gets to go to the competitions with him. This is considered her holiday. The strongman competition schedule has meant that as a couple they have travelled to the Philippines, Dubai, and South Africa. Luke concluded that yes, he must be addicted, but that not all addictions are bad and that being addicted to something that improves your fitness, general well-being, and outlook on life cannot be a bad thing. Luke's justification of his choices did not surprise me. In order to continue with his training schedule and behaviours, he had to justify what he was doing, otherwise he wouldn't be doing it. I wanted to explore whether or not he could see the impact that his "addiction" or obsession was having on those around him.

Luke confirmed that of course his behaviours affect his relationship with his wife and his friends. He had an awareness that what he was doing was all-consuming. On occasion, he and his wife will have dinner booked with friends and Luke will cancel as he has to prioritise his evening gym session. This is indicative of Luke not putting his wife first and this affects their relationship. Despite this, he describes how his wife is quite understanding but that he has had to drill it into her over the years that this is the way it's going to be. Luke confirmed that what he was saying was probably shitty, telling someone that I'm not going to change for you and this is how I am. He told me: "I am a selfish person by saying that, 'This is where I am, if you don't like it fuck off,' maybe not as blunt as that, but in a roundabout way, that's what I'm saying."

Obsessed?

It appeared to be an opportune moment to ask again: so, do you think you're obsessed? "Yeah, I am, why not, I may as well be, I couldn't not be." Luke's hesitation around using the word obsessed related to his fear that obsessed may make him sound a "bit mental" although he went on to say that, "You're hurting and dying when you're training, so you have to be obsessed to do something like that." He told me that he could never be OK with just going in to do a few sets. We all have different internal barometers of what being obsessed with something means. For me, being obsessed with something means that it becomes all-consuming to the exclusion of everything else. I guess in these terms, Luke's training regime could be described as obsessive. He was maintaining a relationship with his wife and work but his training regime confirmed how these things came second.

So, we revisit the question: is this unhealthy? Remember our two criteria for questioning this: one, is the personality trait causing symptoms that cause significant distress or impairment to the individual's social, occupational, or everyday functioning and, two, what happens if the individual stops engaging in the behaviours that are driven by said personality trait? Well, Luke shared with me that his relationship with his wife had almost ended; before Scotland's Strongest Man she had given him an ultimatum and walked away. It was also impacting upon his social life with friends, having to cancel dinners and social events; holidays were also a no go. While competing at World's Strongest Man in the Philippines, Luke's granny died. His flight was delayed by 24 hours and he missed her funeral. He did not see this as acceptable and it was not easy. However, despite all of this, Luke is still with his wife, his friends remain his friends and he is not distressed by not having holidays, in fact he quite likes not having them. Furthermore, he is continuing to function at work and in his everyday life. By this measure, Luke's obsessionality did not appear to have tipped over into something unhealthy for him.

I then asked about what may happen if he didn't train. He told me that he would be angry, frustrated, agitated, and more antsy, on the edge. He told me that he cannot take a step back right now, as he wants to be the best in Scotland, Britain, Europe, and the World.

For Luke, this behaviour was not yet unhelpful to him, it was still functional in helping him achieve his goals. So, what was driving him and why was it that he was obsessed with becoming the strongest man in the world?

Adversity, immigration, and survival

I often find when I speak to athletes that they're not quite sure why they do what they do and why their goals are so important to them. Consciously, in reality, they know, ultimately, that what they are striving to achieve is potentially not really worth all the sacrifice, and asking the "why" question can be quite challenging. If you recall, I put the "why" question to Luke and he struggled to answer it. He certainly is not alone in this. As a psychodynamic psychotherapist, I believe that we are all driven by our unconscious. By the very nature of our unconscious, this means that we do not necessarily know what lives there and what is driving us unless we work with a therapist to explore its contents. Whilst interviewing all of the athletes in this book, I was careful to audio record every conversation, transcribe the interview, and look carefully at the contents of the transcription and the language being used. Revisiting Luke's transcript, I was struck by the language he was using and the repeated reference to adversity in his dialogue.

When describing his current situation, Luke spoke about how proud he was of his achievements despite the challenging situation that he found himself in with his work. He takes great pleasure in beating people who are in a better situation to his that enables them to train full time. In reality, he told me that working offshore means he is only training half the time and he is still beating people.

The area of being comfortable was another fixation point for Luke. He told me that he never likes to feel comfortable in anything he does and he likes to challenge himself. He feels that despite his size, one of his strongest attributes is his mentality. He can go away for work at sea for three weeks, come back and go straight into a competition and win it. He told me it is this quality that he thinks separates him from a lot of people. Luke recalled a conversation with one of the World Strongest Man organisers who asked him when he was going to go full time. To this Luke replied that he couldn't justify it at present. The organiser retorted, "Full-time training, full-time results. Part-time training, part-time results." Luke had just finished 12th in the world and took great pride in this. He had little compassion for people that work Monday to Friday and report that they don't have enough time or energy to go to the gym. He felt this was just making excuses and laziness.

This challenge or adversity seemed to increase in magnitude last year around the time of Scotland's Strongest Man, when his wife walked out the night before the competition. He told me how it was horrendous, she had driven off with all of his kit and food in the back of the car and on the morning of the competition he showed up with nothing but a T-shirt and a pair of flip flops. He thought to himself, "This is what you've got, you've got to deal with it," and begged and stole from all the other competitors. Luke did speak to his wife one hour before the start of the competition. But he had spent four months training and the title meant a lot to him as it was his first competition since his mother passed away. He knew he had a commitment to his wife too, but in that moment, he was competing for himself. He explained that, of course, it may be an added incentive to compete for others but, number one, you have to do it for yourself. For the next five hours of the competition, he switched his mind off, ignored what was going on, and won it. He told me that he couldn't control what was going to happen with his wife but he could control winning the competition.

It appeared that for Luke, unconsciously, there was something about adversity or overcoming challenging circumstances or situations that was a primary motivator for him. It was also what made him feel proud. Earlier in the book, you may recall how I spoke about how often unconscious drivers can be laid down before we are even conceived. These can then be maintained by family narratives and unconscious processes. For Luke, with his Opa in the background, a Polish prisoner of war, I wondered about the transgenerational impact of adversity on Luke. From a very early age, he was aware of adversity, the challenges of life, and how despite these challenges you can still be a respected man of the community. A lot of work has been done in the psychoanalytic community about the transgenerational impact of trauma on first- and second-generation survivors of the Holocaust and collective societal traumas on subsequent generations.[6,7] Salman Akhtar[8] has also written an incredibly helpful book called *Immigration and Acculturation: Mourning, Adaptation, and the Next Generation* (2014) that explores the impact of immigration and culture more widely on our internal worlds.

Luke's mentality had clearly been influenced by his Polish roots and the experiences of his grandfather. With immigration, what can follow is an entirely different attitude to life. For Luke, he had an overwhelming sense of gratitude and disliking for anything entitled. My own grandfather, a Ukrainian prisoner of war, had also started his life in the UK in Inverness. Coming from an immigrant family, there is an awareness that you have to make the most of the opportunity you have been given; there is pressure to succeed to take full advantage of your ancestors' sacrifices, because the alternative could have been an entirely different story. In this instance, it was to be sent back home and be shot. Akhtar talks about the overwhelming sense of high expectations and having to better oneself and climb the social ladder for the next generation of immigrants (pp. 170–171), almost perhaps in fantasy, as if this will protect the individual from anything catastrophic ever happening.

The lack of control experienced by prisoners of war means it is often the case that not having control in one's life can be anxiety provoking. What happens if you step out of line? What happens if you're noticed? Such fate under a dictatorship can be fatal. I was reminded of Luke's dislike for authority figures and how he could never respect his teachers, telling me that he always struggled with how some people just demand respect despite not earning it. Luke also struggled with things being thrown at him last minute. He told me he cannot cope with this as much as he should. Luke gets his training done in the morning and then he can have a good day. If he doesn't, he normally

---

[6] Pines, D. (1993). *A Woman's Unconscious Use of Her Body: A Psychoanalytical Perspective.* London: Routledge, 2010.

[7] Bakó, T., & Zana, K. (2020). *Transgenerational Trauma and Therapy: The Transgenerational Atmosphere.* London: Routledge.

[8] Akhtar, S. (2014). *Immigration and Acculturation: Mourning, Adaptation, and the Next Generation.* Lanham, MD: Rowman & Littlefield.

has a bad day. He likes his routine and doing anything outside the norm makes him feel uncomfortable. When his wife organises seeing her family, this can lead to Luke being in a bad mood as he has already committed to his training schedule.

Obsessionality is, not surprisingly, associated with control and underpinned by anxiety. To be obsessive about something you have to control your daily routine and those around you. Often if this control is lost, it can lead to feelings of anxiety. Remember Luke's earlier comment that if he cannot train for a number of days, he gets panicky? It therefore follows that obsessive-compulsive disorder is considered to be an anxiety disorder. Luke likes his own world and doesn't like venturing out too much. Being in the gym, he feels safe. When he travels, he will always visit the gym and again, he feels safe there. A 20 kg dumb-bell in Scotland is the same as a 20 kg dumb-bell in Asia, he reminded me. It gives him a sense of the familiar and he described the gym as his "wee safe zone".

Despite Luke's protests regarding how he never likes to feel comfortable, here he was telling me that actually, he feels safe when he is comfortable. Akhtar talks about the geographical displacement felt by immigrants once settled in a new country. I wondered again about Luke's grandfather and how displaced he must have felt. For him, his place of safety appeared to be his garden. For Luke, familiarity and safety are to be found in the gym.

Luke confirmed that his grandfather worked hard, kept his head down and just wanted to provide for his family. Luke's appraisal of the UK was one of a benefit state that hosts a cultural group whose members have become entitled and are unfamiliar with a solid work ethic. This frustrates him. His work ethic runs through each and every day and he struggles to relax. If he does relax, he told me that he first has to earn this luxury. He likes reading a nice book, lying in the garden, but he has to have been to the gym first. Relaxation is a reward, not something that he is entitled to.

Luke's career choice was also not far from my mind. He had entered a field that is considered, by many, dangerous. This is why the pay offshore is often considered so high because of the dangers associated to working there. Again, Luke had not opted to choose a career that felt comfortable; he was maintaining an environment much like that of his grandfather's fate, that presented challenge and risk, even if it didn't always consciously feel this way.

Bakó and Zana (2020) talk about how, for the next generations of those that have been traumatised, there is a continued sense or unconscious maintenance of living in a world that poses threat, where the individual feels a need to focus on survival. This becomes a way of being and relating to the world, so that by its very nature the individual will become inwardly focused. There was even risk associated to his strongman dreams. I discussed with Luke Eddie Hall's earlier comment about wanting to become World's Strongest Man or die trying. He was of the opinion that our cardiovascular system can take a lot and he doesn't feel that he would risk dying for his sport but he is happy to risk shortening his life for it. He told me that he would rather have lived and been the best at one point in his life, rather than have lived his life until he was over the age of 100, just living his years out. For Luke, life was finite. He told me that his wife believed in reincarnation, but for him, when you're dead you're dead and so he's going to make the most of the time he has.

Luke's grandfather had published a book about his experiences as a prisoner of war, called *Trust Me, You Will Survive*.[9] Even the title was loaded with how, despite adversity, you will survive. I spoke to Luke about some of the negative physical consequences of sport for athletes and his response was, "But did they die?" Luke's mentality was one where he expected setbacks and hardships. In his words, he expected to get fucked up, break your knee caps, but for a small percentile, they will be able to push on and they won't die. He projected that by the time he was 60 he would probably have to receive double knee replacements and hip replacements but who was to say that he wouldn't have had to have those anyway despite his sport? Luke's sympathetic response to my own experience was, "OK, your appendix burst, fucking hell yeah, you didn't die, but fucking get on with it." We laughed.

This was at the heart of Luke's motivation, what was really driving him. Despite all the adversity and trauma that his grandfather had been exposed to, he had survived. And for Luke, he was continuing to

---

[9] Stoltman, D. (1994). *Trust Me, You Will Survive*. Edinburgh, Scotland: The Pentland Press.

maintain this legacy by overcoming any challenge or adversity that was in his way. He wanted to be remembered as one of the greatest strength athletes in Scotland. I couldn't help but think that his strength was being displayed through his physicality yet, really, Luke's "strength" was all about his mental strength and ability to overcome and ultimately, to survive.

Summary

Obsessionality is a very familiar personality trait that characterises our high-performance athletes. They are indeed skewed to the right. This chapter has explored where obsessionality comes from, whether it be understood in terms of transgenerational trauma, the unconscious need for control, or neuroscience, and how addiction may be understood as a consequence of the development of dopamine pathways over time and the acquisition of behaviours that are rewarding that eventually become habitual. Most likely, it is the interplay between all these factors: social, psychological and biological that contributes to the development and maintenance of obsessional behaviour. With this understanding, we can then start to question where the line is between healthy and unhealthy behaviour.

With Luke's story we explore the impact on others as part of this decision and also how this judgement is individually derived. With regard to mental health we return to our trusty questions; one, does the behaviour cause significant distress or impairment to the individual's social, occupational, or everyday functioning and, two, what happens if the individual stops engaging in the behaviours that are driven by said personality trait. The answers to these questions will again be specific to the individual.

Finally, this chapter has shed light on the biological underpinning of the relationship between exercise, dopamine, mood and addiction and how injury, retirement and seasonal sports should be given thought regarding management of time away from sport, reduced levels of dopamine and the possible consequences of this on mood and mental health.

CHAPTER 5

Focus

F ocus, determination, and obsessiveness can all be seen as close siblings in sport. When one is able to focus on one goal or one sport to the exclusion of everything else it is very possible that this may become obsessive or a form of avoidance of something else. Obsessionality has, however, been thought about in more depth already; it is not my intention to reiterate that material here. Instead, I wish to think about how focus, a quality so celebrated in sport, can also become so skewed to the right that it is functional on the field, yet less so off. Cricket is a sport that relies on one's ability to focus, there is no doubting this. The batsman has to focus on the ball and the ball alone in order to make contact and deliver runs. The fielder has to focus on the ball to catch the opposing team's batting efforts. And the bowler has to focus on the stumps.

Cricket is gruelling in this sense, hours upon hours focusing on a small, red, leather ball. Once the individual is functioning within the realms of professional cricketer, the magnitude of their need to focus increases, as the number of distractions escalates: the increasing size of the crowds and the increasing internal pressure to perform for oneself and for one's team. Sports psychologists are often commissioned to support cricketers (and other athletes) to hone their skills in the art of focus. Whilst an essential skill on the field, if it becomes a pervasive personality trait where parts of one's internal world become switched off, it can lead to difficulties elsewhere. The very nature of skilled focus is the exclusion or avoidance of other things, not only in one's external environment but also in one's internal environment (or mind). It requires an incredible ability to switch off. Freud warned of the potential for neuroses if people avoid their internal struggles for too long. The relationship between focus, avoidance, denial, and pathology is complex, and one that I wanted to explore with Graeme Fowler, the England cricketer.

Graeme Fowler was an international cricketer who played for his country from 1982 to 1986. He has struggled with depression since 2004 and has spoken openly about this across many platforms. He has now written two books that also detail his struggles: *Absolutely Foxed* and *Mind Over Batter*. His experiences have also afforded him the opportunity to work with the Professional Cricketers Association (PCA) as a mental health ambassador working to raise awareness of mental health difficulties in the sport.

Graeme is physically quite a noticeable character. At the age of 59 (when I interviewed him), he is a man of slight stature but offers one of the most voluminous grey beards among his peers. Something that I sense has become part of his character along with his selection of thick-framed circular glasses. He continues to dress in a way which may be described as anything but understated, always including colour and pattern. His e-cigarette is never far from his side and hence he is often surrounded by a translucent veil of synthetic smoke. Graeme told me that all throughout his cricketing career, and to this day, he had dressed in a flamboyant way to get himself noticed. He could be easily recognised on tour and he stood out as being different. This was part of a jokey role that he would play. He told me that most people didn't even realise that he had a brain until he finished playing cricket and wrote for *The Sunday Telegraph*.

Family background and early experiences

Graeme grew up in the family home with his mother, father, and sister until he left home to go to university at the age of 18. He told me that he did not get on with his mother or his sister but his father was one of the most generous people he had ever met. His father's previous wife had died and Graeme's mother was his father's second wife. She used to be friends with his father's first wife. His mother was highly strung and she would walk past Graeme and hit him for no reason. This would happen on frequent occasions until, at the age of 16, she hit Graeme on the head with a heavy catalogue and when she attempted to hit him a second time, he was able to overpower her by holding her arms. His mother would often do these things and then want to cuddle him afterwards. It is a pattern that continues into the present day where she asks Graeme to cuddle her and give her his love. This made and continues to make no sense to Graeme.

Graeme thought that his relational experiences with his mother were normal. Much like Michelle, earlier in the book, this had become Graeme's template position which he had come to accept and had internalised. He would go to school and be beaten there (at this point, corporal punishment was legal in Great Britain) and he would go home and be beaten there too. At school, Graeme was mischievous and thought that perhaps he was asking for it on occasions. His sister was his half-sister and they never got along. They still do not get along to this very day. Graeme's relationship with his father, however, seemed different. He described him as a generous man who wanted something better for Graeme. Despite this, he was never able to give Graeme any compliments. If Graeme got 19 out of 20 in a spelling test, his father would ask him why he didn't get 20 out of 20. His father worked hard and so was less available to Graeme in the home during the day, and also one suspects was unavailable to protect him from his mother's behaviour. His dad never refused to play with him, though, and at lunchtime Graeme would walk home from school and play football with his dad before returning to afternoon lessons. It was his father who first introduced him to cricket on one of their family holidays. Graeme wanted to buy a cricket bat with his pocket money. His father told him that he could have any bat he wanted on two conditions: that he used it and that he looked after it. Graeme still has his first cricket bat.

In a selection of old photographs that Graeme shared, my attention was captured by two small photos. One showed what I initially thought to be a young girl in a dress. I was told that this was in fact Graeme at the age of 11 in his mother's wedding dress going to a fancy-dress party.

When I asked why his mother had dressed him in that way, Graeme felt that perhaps she did not want to go to the effort of making an outfit for him. Graeme found this funny and so too did everyone else at the party. He didn't seem to mind this, as at the age of six or seven he first realised that he was actually quite good at making other people laugh. He even recalls doing something funny or cheeky on occasions even though he knew he might get hit by his mum for doing it. A further extension of Graeme's template role was now that of the Joker. This appeared to be one way for Graeme to express his aggression towards his mother, which, in turn, resulted in her hitting him for his cheek or mischievous nature. In complete contrast, I then found a very tender picture of Graeme sitting at the feet of his father, leaning up against him. I noted a real difference in Graeme's posture and he seemed at ease and safe in this image. It was his favourite place to sit in the family sitting room and this was where he regularly placed himself, as he did not want to be near his mother or sister.

As a child, Graeme wanted to be one of two things: a pilot or someone who built bridges. For many children who experience challenging family environments, the dream of an alternative, loving relationship or flying away is not uncommon. He went on to explain, however, that he needed maths to be a pilot or an engineer and he wasn't any good at maths so he was screwed and didn't know what to do. All Graeme knew was that he wanted to get away from his mother and with cricket he knew that he could go to Australia. He completed a Certificate of Education at Durham University and didn't go back for his fourth year to gain a bachelor's degree as he went to play cricket instead.

After his professional cricketing career, Graeme returned to Durham University to set up Durham's centre of excellence where he would coach for the next 20 years of his life. He told me that during this time he was approached by a woman studying for a PhD at the university, who asked if she could administer a test to all his cricketers. Graeme responded that if she wanted to do this test with his lads, then he was going to do it first.

He met with the researcher in his office and she informed me that she wanted to administer a test used with Swedish fighter pilots to see if they could detect danger. The researcher proceeded to black out Graeme's office with bin liners and told him to look into a microscope.

He was informed that images would flash in front of his eyes and he just needed to say what he saw. Graeme told me that he looked down the microscope and couldn't see anything but the researcher told him to just keep going. As the test continued, he started to respond, with some uncertainty, "Oh, that's a bike, that's a trumpet, and that's a man playing a guitar" and he thought nothing of it. At the end of the test, the researcher switched the lights on and asked if he had always had such a difficult relationship with his mother.

Graeme was astounded that the researcher had managed to deduce this from his responses. He confirmed that she had beaten him and that he had just learned to block everything out. Her response was that perhaps it was this skill that had made him the batsman he was. Graeme's experience of being beaten at home had in effect allowed him to hone the skill of switching off and focusing. Graeme was really disturbed by what the researcher had told him for the entirety of the week following the test, and he told her that she wasn't going to be testing his athletes.

Graeme's struggle with depression

In 2004, Graeme experienced his first episode of depression. This was ten years after he finished playing cricket and everything was "perfect". The centre was successful, he had three children, a nice home, and his wife, Sarah. He was doing fine. Then, it just hit him, seemingly out of nowhere. He had searched many a time to find a trigger for its onset but had come up empty time and time again. The only thing he could come up with was that his mind had had enough of being abused and it wanted a rest. To Graeme, it didn't matter if he could find a trigger or not, what mattered to him was the future. This was what he focused on instead. He associated this mentality to his sporting days, explaining that he had never focused on endings and instead would focus on how something else was starting. Even at the point when Graeme's employment at Durham University was coming to an end after 20 years, he was not focusing on the ending, but how, instead, he was going to start working with the Professional Cricketers' Association (PCA) on raising awareness of mental health difficulties.

Graeme's constant focus on moving forwards meant that he never looked back or connected with the emotional content of endings and loss. Winnicott,[10] one of our pioneer psychoanalysts, reminds us that with every new development there must be a loss. And, with loss, one must process it and adjust to the variety of feelings that may accompany it. This may include denial, anger, sadness, and depression, eventually allowing an individual to move to reintegration and acceptance. Instead, Graeme described a process of just moving on to the next.

Perhaps Graeme had moved through his life at such a pace, always on to the next thing, without fully processing loss, uncertainty, and emotional distress, that he was disconnected from the emotional contents of his mind. Graeme had a complex relationship to loss, though. He explained that on the day he was picked to play for England, he knew there would be a day when he would be dropped. He had always seen the end at the start of something and he had actually become very skilled at analysing loss on a daily basis at the end of a game. His analysis, however, was a tactical or intellectual one, it did not involve any emotional processing.

Graeme felt that perhaps the only reason for the onset of his depression was because his mind had given up. Constantly defending against our internal worlds does come at a price and it will inevitably deplete our egos. The ego for Freud[11] is the part of our personality that tries to balance our innate drives (id) alongside our internalised morals (superego). Perhaps Graeme's ego had had enough after constantly fighting or defending against his inner struggles for so long and he fell into a depression as a consequence. Perhaps for the first time in ten years, when things were going well in his life, he did not have to be in a defensive position where he had to fight (much like on the cricket pitch). He told me that this was a familiar position for him. If we recall his template role, he was always the one that was being beaten. Graeme told me he had become the person that was always getting up off the floor. If this wasn't being maintained in Graeme's external world, his internal world was going to deliver it for him. Graeme confirmed that for him failure was easier to do than success and that maintaining success is the hardest thing.

---

[10] Winnicott, D. W. (1958). *Collected Papers: Through Paediatrics to Psychoanalysis*. London: Tavistock.
[11] Freud, S. (1923b). *The Ego and the Id. S. E., 19*. London: Hogarth.

Graeme's struggle connecting with the emotional contents of his mind, something that had served him very well on the field, meant that accessing therapy was not on the cards for him. Instead, he managed his depression with a significant amount of medication. This made him feel numb, which was better than wanting to be dead. Depression can affect people's internal worlds very differently, and for Graeme it meant that he had no interest in anything. He loved humour—remember his mischievous and cheeky side—yet his kids would put on comedy DVDs and Graeme didn't want to watch. If he did sit and watch, they just weren't funny. He loved going outside but he simply could not go out; for a period of four weeks, he didn't go through an external door. By this stage, Graeme would sit and stare at a Land Rover magazine all day, and it was the same magazine day after day. He described it as the shutters going down, that the TV was on standby, the light was on but nothing was happening.

When his family were out during the day he would just lie on his sofa and it didn't matter if the TV was on or not, he would just stare as if something of his mind had been switched off. To him, it felt like he was paralysed, at times wanting to get a cup of tea and not being able to get up off the sofa to make it. He dreaded the return of his family at the end of the day as he couldn't talk, he had no words in his head, he was blank. At one point he recalls being told by his wife that he hadn't spoken to anyone for four weeks. Graeme's depression was characterised by a switching off of his mind. There was no mention of any feeling or affect.

In the back of his mind somewhere, Graeme thought, "This is just a chemical imbalance." As already considered in Chapter Four on obsessionality, the neurotransmitters in our brain play a role in mood but these are not mutually exclusive to our behaviours, our thoughts, and the emotional contents of our thoughts. One will inevitably impact upon the other. Despite chemical treatment assisting with management of low mood in the short term, it should, if possible, be used as an adjunct to talking therapy that will in time lead to a longer-term outcome, that will allow for tapering of medication so a dependency is not built up over the long term.

Graeme explained that all he had ever known was cricket and that within every match the game would ebb and flow and he started to apply this to his mental health, something that proved helpful to him. Just like in his batting career he started to recognise better and worse days. He became more patient with his mind, but still did not wish to explore the emotional content of it. Instead, he would remind himself that it was just a chemical imbalance and that there was no other reason for the symptoms he was experiencing. Historically, when physically injured during his professional career, he used to reassure himself that he just had to pass the time until he would be well again. He struggled on these occasions but eventually his physical injuries would mend. He anticipated that it would be the same with his mental health, just longer. This was not the case.

Graeme explained that he had always chosen to be on the edge or on the periphery of something. He preferred it this way. He had never really followed the crowd and had chosen to live his life in this disconnected way. To become a successful sportsman, he had to develop a resilience or a stubbornness where he had to focus and ignore everything else. Before he was selected for first team cricket, he had four operations on his feet and he had to learn how to walk again. To do this he disconnected from the pain and the reality of the situation and knew he just had to do it. He lived in his own head and in his own life. Being disconnected from his emotions was therefore helpful as he never felt guilty about missing his best mate's wedding, for instance, if he had to train or compete. He described himself as "incredibly selfish" and even after two divorces, he was grateful that he still had himself.

Graeme could not talk about everything as this would "take the lid off the can of worms". It appeared that he was fearful of engaging in a talking therapy and what he might find in the contents of his conscious and unconscious world. It was too overwhelming. For every patient we must respect that there are limits to what they wish to explore and this is not something that should be forced. This is one of the reasons why, in psychoanalysis, the patient leads the contents of the session.

Graeme's treatment of choice, medication, allowed him to manage his symptoms yet also allowed him to maintain a position where he remained disconnected from the internal struggles in his mind. In the depths of his depression, Graeme instinctively knew that he didn't want to talk to anyone. He wanted to deal with it himself. At this point, I was sitting across from Graeme in the Fowlers' garden room, and I couldn't help but notice the *British National Formulary* (BNF) staring at me pointedly on their family bookcase, albeit as part of a wider eclectic collection, including multiple books on bridges. It was unusual to see such a book on your average family bookcase. The BNF is a pharmaceutical reference guide on the selection and clinical use of medicines, more commonly seen on the desk of one's GP. Instead, not one, but two of these books seemed at home nestling on Graeme's bookshelf.

After a while on his medication, Graeme wanted to start to connect again, but without the use of an emotional language Graeme resorted to the use of numbers. He introduced a 1–20 scale. The number 10 equates to "OK", anything below "10" is struggling and anything above 10 communicates that he is doing well. Graeme confirmed that his head was logical and practical, certainly not emotional. Words did not form in his mind, and in his household they have a saying that no one can spell the word sympathy. These foundations were laid early on as a child for Graeme. His mother's response to pain or injury was a practical one, there would be no hug or language to comfort. Graeme didn't feel that this was solely a failing of his family home: he described that culturally in the 1960s, school, society, and life in general wasn't emotional.

Graeme frequently joked about how his wife and he were very similar and that she would also operate in a very logical way. Graeme and Sarah were a good fit because for whatever reason they both have an emotional part of them that is shut off and a logical, concrete part of them that is very much present in their everyday lives. His wife struggled to understand Graeme's depression initially as she "didn't do emotions". A logical, non-emotional exchange was therefore established between the two of them in order to communicate where his internal mind was. Sarah would look at Graeme and ask if he wanted anything, she would then ask what number he was, Graeme would respond and Sarah would say "OK".

Graeme's second depressive episode occurred exactly ten years after his first in 2014. This time he had an obvious trigger, a drawn-out battle about the future of his position with the centre for excellence at Durham University. More than ever, when Graeme spoke about this experience, he seemed connected with a real concern and anger about the potential downfall of what he had created over so many years. Something that he had clearly invested a lot of his time and energy into. He raged that

"It takes a long time to build a wall and it takes one dickhead with a hammer to knock it all down." In psychoanalysis we often think about symbolism in people's communication and with this comment I wondered if Graeme was not only referring to the centre of excellence that he feared was about to be knocked down, but also his defensive inner wall that cut him off from his emotions. This was something that took a lot of his energy and resources to maintain yet the actions of one individual were able to break this down and send him spiralling into another episode of depression.

On stage

Spending time with Graeme, you start to realise what a captivating storyteller he is. This is not only in his demeanour but also in the material he talks about. It was clear that Graeme had lived a colourful life and that his earlier reference to the "ebb and flow" of a cricket game was a fitting metaphor. The ebbs and flows, mind you, did not seem to be something that would be found on your average tidal river; instead he seemed to be describing something of much greater magnitude. Graeme could describe not only the deep depressive troughs in his life but also the highest of peaks.

In his cricketing career, there were many peaks, including scoring a century versus West Indies at Lord's in 1984 and being the first Englishman to score a double century (201 runs) in India at Madras in 1985. Graeme liked the external feedback that he got from the men that watched him play; he was quick to identify that this positive feedback was not something he received at home. Alongside his cricketing career, Graeme also took up modelling. He was asked to model sports clothes for catalogues and was signed up to the Pamela Holt Agency. He liked being on show, being on stage.

Graeme had been close friends with Elton John once upon a time and had partied in Perth and on huge superyachts. He loved to play the drums and he and a number of sportsmen and musicians called the Mark Butcher Band put on a concert at the Royal Albert Hall at the PCA dinner three years in a row. As is consistent with Graeme's disconnection with his emotional mind, it takes a lot for him to get an adrenaline rush. Many times in the past, and as recent as 2007,

Graeme had climbed up the outside of buildings to prove a point or to play pranks on his fellow team mates, scattering crisps on their beds and escaping off the balcony scaling sheer drops. He had also jumped out of a 23rd floor window in Delhi. It had a concrete ledge running around the building approximately as wide as a side table, so he crouched outside the window on his haunches and as he could hear his teammates behind him saying "What's Foxy doing? Get him off, get him off," he said "Bye!" and jumped out. His teammates screamed and looked out of the window to see Graeme had landed on another ledge and was laughing. He then ran around the building on the ledge. Graeme also likes skydiving and has done this three times. On one occasion he was sitting by the open door in the plane, not yet attached to his instructor, when the plane banked. He almost fell out and this petrified him. He has never been the same with heights since.

On Wikipedia, Graeme has been described as the "joker in the dressing room", yet he told me that this was "a load of shit really". Despite this, he confirmed that he was familiar with playing a role and hiding behind it. When on tour in Auckland everyone asked him where they should go out. He would go out with three lads one night and another three lads the next night, but when he wanted a night off, his teammates wouldn't let him. He quickly realised that if he made out he was seeing a female friend, he would get a night off. He would tell the lads that he had a bit of business, wander out to have a drink on his own, and wander back to the hotel when there was no one there. He would go to his room, order room service and just be on his own. He wanted a night off from performing and the next morning the lads would ask him how he got on. Their imagination was greater than the actual reality. This maintained Graeme's need to be somewhat on the edge, to always be slightly disconnected from the group.

There is a concept in psychoanalysis called the "false self" as described by Winnicott.[12] This is something that is created as part of one's personality when a child feels it is safer to comply with the demands of the caregivers in their environment in order to keep themselves safe.

---

[12] Winnicott, D. W. (1986). *Home Is Where We Start from: Essays by a Psychoanalyst*. C. Winnicott, R. Shepard, & M. Davis (Eds.). New York: W. W. Norton.

It then creates a certain way of being in front of others. The concept was later developed and described as a "caretaker self" rather than a false self, which actually seeks to look after the person until a time when they feel able to let the seeds of the real self grow. Graeme could relate to this idea and confirmed that he possesses a mask, that this is who he is most of the time, when he is doing a talk at a dinner, when he is broadcasting. However, when his depression hit, he could no longer act.

People can get somewhat tied up in their thinking about the false self and the real self and I think the term "false self" is somewhat unfortunate in helping us to think about the concept because of the instant negative associations to this. It is not intended in this way. Instead, perhaps Graeme's mask is more helpful to think about. For him this was experienced as something that he learned to wear, much like his colourful shirts. Over time he realised that he received positive feedback from those around him for being outrageous, for being mischievous and for being a character. This was internalised and these behaviours were reinforced and therefore maintained. Many people ask if their "false self" is then actually their real self because it has been a part of them for so long. I think this is a valid point. However, I would argue that the "false self" does become part of one's personality structure but more as a defensive mask on top of what lies underneath.

In Graeme's case, as is the case for many sportsmen and women, performing at such a high level offers a huge amount of external feedback about how good they are at something and this should be celebrated. Of course, what is missing is feedback for being valued for just being, without having to achieve and perform. The individual then struggles to establish this internally and they are driven to perform or achieve in order to feel that they are valued. Under these circumstances, the individual is left on shaky ground, as they become dependent on external feedback to boost their self-confidence and worth. When this is lost, what may be found is something more fragile and uncertain.

This fits with Graeme's upbringing: he had a father who he wished was more available to him to offer him the feedback that he was a valued son. Instead, he seemed to find this in the other men that would spectate on the side line at the cricket club. His mother's attacking behaviour inevitably did not communicate worth, love, and value to Graeme and so by disconnecting his emotional mind, focusing on performing on the cricket pitch, and to others off the pitch with his mask on, he was able to derive some positive feedback. This of course is only a temporary solution to the problem and when the temporary feedback found throughout the cricket season is lost, Graeme slips into a depression.

The end of the summer season

I had visited Graeme on a few occasions to complete his interviews. One September morning after our initial meeting I returned to finish our discussions. The man I found was an entirely different Graeme. He had been on holiday with his family and had experienced a bit of a wobble a few days prior to my arrival. September coincidentally marked the end of the summer season, something of an internalised rhythm that Graeme still responded to, dating back to his days as a professional cricketer.

If you recall, earlier in the book, I spoke of how we now have a biological understanding as to why low mood may set in during low season for cricketers (or any other athlete): as training and competing ends, so too does their endless supplies of dopamine in the brain which is produced during exercise. Graeme had now retired, but his career post-retirement was coaching, so this rhythm of increased activity during the cricket season had continued for him. With the end of the season, Graeme had simultaneously taken down a tent and a tepee in the back garden that he sleeps in during the summer and instead he would now have to sleep inside the house for the autumn and winter months. There was a sense of disappointment and loss. I too felt disappointed as I had hoped to take a picture of his tent and tepee in the garden, and this opportunity was no more. I had thought that the tent and the tepee symbolised something so important to Graeme that I was keen to capture this shot and make sure that it made its way into the book when photographs were going to be included. Instead, we went outside and what was left were two large areas of blackened soil where the grass now lay dead. The ground sheet and tarpaulin were hanging over the washing line and the tent pegs and poles lay in a bag next to the side of the house.

As much as I was disappointed, instead, I was privileged to see something different of Graeme in this visit. Without having ventured outside into the garden and the fields that surrounded Graeme's property, I don't think I would have truly appreciated the significance of being outside to Graeme and the loss of the summer season. In summer, Graeme was alive, his mask was firmly attached and I was captivated by his storytelling and showbiz type stories of how Elton John had historically queried how much Graeme's contract was worth in hope that he may be able to buy him out to offer him a new position as his friend on tour. Graeme was alive and captivating in his storytelling and he was connected to a time that was full of life, drama, and elation.

In September, Graeme took me to a small graveyard and sat on the bench overlooking the headstones and the fields and told me that this is where he goes when he is struggling. He explained that it was unfortunate that it was not pissing it down (colloquial term for heavy rain) because he liked the rain. He would often put his cagoule on, walk outside and sit in the rain. He loved the rain but this was ironic really because he hates deep water. I realised that deep water and taking the lid off the box were synonymous to Graeme and that what he was referring to was going inside himself and how this may elicit fear in what he may find in the deep inner water within him.

Historically, when he played cricket, walking onto the pitch was his sanctuary; he could focus on the game in hand and ignore everything else in his mind. He hated half past six at night as he would then have to deal with stuff. It appeared that Graeme's tent and tepee were a potential attempt at rebuilding a sanctuary outside; his desire to find solace again in the summer season of switching off on the cricket field where he could focus and sit outside the inner demons in his mind. In the winter months, when the cricket pitches are no longer played on, Graeme is no longer distracted, his dopamine levels drop and the shutters start to close in Graeme's mind as he has to move deeper inside and shut the doors to the outside world.

Graeme is able to connect with how his life has always had a feeling of melancholy to it, yet he has never been able to make sense of this. He perceives himself to have had a good life, to have experienced incredible things, never really experienced much loss, and has had jobs that have paid the bills. It seems incomprehensible to Graeme that he should in any way be allowed to connect with anything troubling that may be lurking somewhere inside him. This is not uncommon for people who may have experienced difficult upbringings. The experience seems minimised in the mind of the individual, perhaps in the hope of protecting themselves from connecting with the painful reality of what did happen, or perhaps because the experience was such an everyday experience, why would anyone see it as contributing to anything troublesome? Graeme talks openly about the many disconnections in his life and his logical mind that would locate the past in the past: that was then, he's over it now.

What next?

It is at times of injury or retirement that sportspeople are most commonly known to struggle. In the introduction I reference how our professional sportspeople are placed on a pedestal, idolised, and receive an incredible amount of positive feedback from thousands of others. When this is gone, it is understandable that sportspeople will crash: their external stabilisers that have been keeping them propped up are taken away and they have to navigate the newfound uncertainty and instability of not being propped up in this way anymore.

Post-retirement, Graeme had attempted to maintain his familiar template of being the cheeky and mischievous joker that kept a distance from emotion and focused on the logical and practical. He had morphed himself into a coach and now he seemed to be transitioning into the role of a mental health ambassador. Graeme has been a part of the shift in athletes starting to talk about their own experiences with mental health. Cricket as a profession is now one of the leading sports offering support to their players. For someone like Graeme, as with other sportspeople that are known as big sports personalities, it will of course be a struggle to move away from this. This is who they have become, it is their identity. He had been known as Graeme "Foxy" Fowler for so long and had even created a clothing brand "Fox and Beard". Now, Graeme told me that he was "famous for being a looney". He was introduced to Twitter many years ago and he now has around 15,500 followers. This is his new platform, or stage, to talk about mental health issues and his life. In his dark times it offers him such comfort to know that someone is still out there observing, watching the game. In the high times, he tells me that the responses he receives on Twitter are like verbal applause. Twitter is his new stage. It makes him feel appreciated and validated.

Summary

The ability to focus is, arguably, a necessary prerequisite for any sportsperson wishing to reach the top of their game. It is not uncommon for many professional sportspeople to be described as selfish as a consequence of the extent to which they focus on their individual sporting goals. The choices that the sportsperson has to make, sidelining or sacrificing, can have significant fallout: divorce, loss of friendship, loss of work, loss of social life. For Graeme, however, focusing on cricket and his sporting goals meant that it allowed him to continue to live a disconnected life, on the edge or the periphery of the group and relationships. His focus on sport resulted in incredible successes, yet it also facilitated the avoidance of his past and the emotional contents of his internal world. When he no longer had a focus or something to fight against, he collapsed into a depression with no emotional language owing to his lengthy disconnect.

The impact of the loss of focus on sport must be acknowledged as a point of vulnerability for high-performance sportspeople. The impact of injury and retirement is considered further in Chapter Seven.

Part III

Skewed to the left?

CHAPTER 6

Acceptance

Thus far, I have explored a number of traits that I believe to be skewed to the right in our high-performance sporting population. In other words, they possess high levels of these traits: obsessionality, masochism, and focus. I now want to turn my attention to one trait that I often see in athletes that is not skewed to the right but is actually skewed to the left. This is to say that it is common for me to meet with athletes who have low levels of acceptance and internal worth when compared to the typical population.

I have already spoken about how, for many an athlete, much of their motivation can come from chasing external feedback which offers them a visible measure of their abilities or self-worth. For individuals content with themselves who have been given the same consistent message that they hold value, are good enough and accepted by others without having to perform, they would likely have little motivation to push for more and to prove themselves.

Conversely, when individuals struggle to accept themselves, or a part of themselves, and doubt their internal value, it is very possible that an internal drive to collect measures of their worth is experienced. This offers tangible, external feedback that they are "good" or are valuable. When I refer to *internal value*, I refer to something within the individual that is content with the very nature of who they are as a person. This is more about personal beliefs, values, personality structure, and who someone is as a being, rather than how many certificates, qualifications, money, or trophies they possess. For many a sportsperson, once retirement hits, the clue that low acceptance and internal worth may be lurking in the background somewhere is the ongoing need to collect achievements or accolades in other sports or pursuits. We often see how an athlete goes from one professional sport to another when they retire.

In April 2019, James Cracknell, at the age of 46, returned to Cambridge University to take on the role of student, so as to take part in the Oxford and Cambridge Boat Race. For a large proportion of media and spectators, Cracknell was heralded as a hero for conquering such a sporting achievement at this age. One article however, written by Andrew Anthony of *The Guardian*, reported "James Cracknell's milestone is not sport but masochism in search of meaning". The article confirmed that James's achievement was "super bloody human" but it also invited the reader to consider what "mindset he's fleeing from".

I cannot comment on James Cracknell's personal history but what is noticeable is Cracknell's persistent and relentless pursuit of external achievement after external achievement. Since leaving rowing he has raced across Antarctica to reach the South Pole, completed the toughest foot race on earth, the Marathon des Sables, a six-day, 156-mile ultramarathon run in the Moroccan desert, completed the 2,500 nautical mile transatlantic rowing race with partner, Ben Fogle, and in his attempt to race across America in 18 days by running, cycling and rowing he sustained a life-threating brain injury.

There is no doubt that struggling to accept oneself for who one is and having a poor sense of internal worth is a wonderful motivator to work hard and to achieve more. In this chapter, I hope to explore the vulnerability associated to this presentation. To do this, I spoke with Nigel Owens. Nigel has spoken openly and frequently about his own inability to accept a part of himself, namely his sexuality, and the impact that this has had and continues to have on his mental health. We will now explore his personal story in more detail. For many a Nigel Owens fan, much of his story will be very familiar. However, I hope to offer a new understanding regarding the psychology behind Nigel's story and how his challenge with accepting a part of himself is, in the sporting population, very familiar. He is not alone.

Background

Nigel was born and raised on a council estate in Mynyddcerrig, Carmarthenshire, Wales in the 1970s. Mynyddcerrig is a small rural village that means "Mountain of Stone". At that time it had a population of around 140 people. He lived for the first five years of his life with his parents and grandparents until his parents got a council house. His first five years, living with his parents in his grandparents' home, were on a smallholding of around seven or eight acres. His grandfather was a coal miner and kept cows, chickens and pigs to keep the family going. The family then rented another 10 or 12 acres to home his grandmother's horses. Nigel's father and grandfather used to break in horses and Nigel would get on the horses as they were breaking them in.

At the time of Nigel's birth, his grandfather had a "massive stroke" and was in hospital at the same time as Nigel's mother. His grandmother put Nigel in his grandfather's arms as she thought he might never get to hold him again. The next day his grandfather improved and lived for a further 13 years. Nigel's father was going to sell the horses when his father had the stroke. However, once he came out of the hospital the decision was made to keep them. Farming is a mainstay of Nigel's upbringing and we will later come to learn that it has been reintroduced in Nigel's life more recently.

Nigel was one of 14 children in his local primary school, looked after by two teachers. His first language was Welsh and he spoke no English until the age of six or seven years old when he was taught it in school. The community was small and everybody knew everyone else. On average, there were five to eight children in each family and a lot of children stayed in the village longer term. Nigel was an only child; his parents had him quite late when his father was in his forties and his mother was in her thirties. Family was important and close knit and he describes his upbringing as a happy one. His immediate family home was old-fashioned. As a child he would go to chapel and Sunday school. He was brought up to be respectful, to say please and thank you, and with a clear understanding of right and wrong. Sunday school also reinforced these lessons about morals and the way that one should live life. His parents taught him that when you grow up you have a girlfriend, get married and have children, and this was the way of the world. This is how the world keeps going around.

Nigel passed his 11-plus exams and went on to grammar school. This was a huge change, moving from a school with 14 children to a school with 1,000 children. This was a massive culture shock and one that he describes as the "scariest day of [his] life". For approximately five or six months when he first arrived, Nigel was bullied by one individual; there appeared to be no specific reason for this. At the time, he felt ashamed and weak. He thought the bullying was his fault and that there was something wrong with him. He did not speak out about it and it was affecting his life. For the first time he was doing things he was not brought up to do. He was lying to his parents, saying he was ill and that he did not want to go to school. This did not sit comfortably. The bullying stopped by chance one day when one of his friends saw it happening, clocked the bully and sent him flying to the floor in tears. Nigel then had a choice as to whether or not he should stay at the grammar school or go to the medium (English speaking) school. His friend that hit the bully went to the medium school so Nigel followed him there. Life would have been very different if he had stayed. Defining moments in Nigel's life took place whilst at this next school.

At the age of 14, Nigel was working as a presenter on the TV channel, S4C, and he was also on stage at a local working men's club doing stand-up comedy. Acting, performing and drama was something that Nigel enjoyed. He would often perform in primary schools singing as part of Sunday school activities. His ambition at the time was to appear live on the *Antiques Roadshow*. At the age of 15, Nigel had a different ambition to be a vet. He believes he was far from intelligent enough and so decided to work on a farm instead, thinking that being a farmer would be the next-best thing. His family only had a smallholding though, and so if he wanted his dream to be realised he would have to marry a farmer's daughter. He knew that this would not happen so he put it on hold.

At the age of 16, Nigel had only passed two O Levels and he went back to do A Levels in drama, history and Welsh. The only basis on which he was allowed to go back was if he did resits. He had returned to school for three weeks when the headmaster told Nigel that he'd best make the most of playing rugby that day as the school had to close. Apparently, the school caretaker was no longer able to fulfil his role. Nigel went to visit the headmaster in his office and suggested that Nigel open up the school instead. The headmaster liaised with the education department which agreed to Nigel taking the caretaker job while he completed his education. Nigel was then responsible for opening and locking up and stoking the fires. He was now receiving £138.40 cash in hand each week in 1987. Nigel thought, "Bugger the education, I'm going to take the caretaker job." In a year's time he had left education and was on the Youth Training Scheme and went to work on a farm. He studied agriculture two days a week and then spent five days a week on the farm. The headmaster of the school then asked if Nigel would do the technician's job. He accepted and worked there for the next 13 years.

Nigel first became interested in rugby in 1977 when he was six years old and recalls watching Phil Bennett score one of the greatest tries in history at Murrayfield. He scored the try, put the ball down on the grass under the post and rested his chin on the ball. Nigel then went to the field near his house and recreated the try with a brown leather ball running around the two donkeys, Chocolate and Fudge, and laying on the ball himself. This is when he fell in love with the game. In his primary school there were only two boys of his age so they had to join up with another school to play in their rugby team.

Nigel was a prop in primary school; he described how he was "quite chubby" and his nickname was "Pugsley" as he looked like the character Pugsley from *The Adams Family* on TV. At the age of 12–13 he was playing as a full back at the medium school. His playing career was short-lived when he stepped up to the plate at the age of 16 to take a match deciding conversion and missed this in spectacular fashion. His teacher, John Binham, at the time exclaimed, "Bloody hell, Nigel, will you go and referee or something!" He then refereed for the first time at the age of 16 at local school fixtures and enjoyed it. His interest in refereeing had begun. On Saturdays, Nigel would referee a match and his father would watch him referee while his mother stayed at home and cooked in the kitchen all day. On the way home, they would stop off for a beer and then return home to food. This was considered to be a perfect day.

At the age of 18 or 19, Nigel was starting to realise that he was different to, in his words, "what [he] was supposed to be". He started to notice on occasions that he was attracted to men. This was totally alien to him. In the past, he had had a girlfriend. He had grown up in a rural community where he did not yet know much about the wider world. He did not grow up in a big city where he felt it may have been easier to come to terms with his sexuality. In his small rural community, he felt that he was an island.

There were only 14 in his primary school and unless he got incredibly lucky, it was very unlikely that another individual would have been gay, could have validated his sexuality, and given him a human connection. Nigel had never met anyone who was gay and the only reference point was the stereotyped characters portrayed on TV at the time. Nigel observed this and knew this wasn't him, so he could not make sense of his feelings towards the same sex. At 14 years of age he recalls his cousin asking his father what a "homo" was. His father did not know and told the child to ask Nigel's mother. She replied that she thought it was something to do with washing powder. His parents knew so little about homosexuality and this contributed to things being very difficult for Nigel.

The superego

Earlier in the book (Chapter Five—Focus) you may recall reference to Freud's theory of personality structure.[13] Freud believed that our personality consists of three parts, the id, the ego and the superego. The id references our instinctual drives: we are driven to seek pleasure, food and sex. The superego is our moral compass that we develop throughout our lives where we learn about social norms and rules. It deems what we feel to be acceptable and not acceptable. In this way, the superego is an incredibly important part of our personality that balances out our desire to be constantly pleasure-seeking mammals. For example, children learn quite quickly, with external feedback from parents or others, that it is not acceptable to consume sweets all the

---

[13] Freud, S. (1923b). *The Ego and the Id. S. E., 19.* London: Hogarth.

time and that they must limit this. As adults we also learn very quickly about the social norms regarding sex, consent and what is socially acceptable. If the superego was not in place restricting our behaviour, the id would likely take over.

People's superegos are developed throughout their entire life. The foundation for one's superego is, however, laid down in our childhood. We are exposed to various parental figures, media and peers that provide feedback on what is expected of us and what is acceptable and not acceptable. This information along with those experiences where lessons were learnt stick and become "internalised". To say that something has become internalised is to say that these beliefs become a part of the very fabric of who we are. Some may be very much in our conscious awareness but others may be in our unconscious, outside our awareness but still, ultimately, defining how we behave in an automatic way.

For Nigel, his early development and experiences growing up with parents and grandparents in the small Welsh rural community of Mynyddcerrig meant that his superego was shaped in a very particular way. If you recall, the accepted narrative was one where you grow up, get a girlfriend, get married and have children, and this is how the world keeps turning. For Nigel, however, his id was in absolute conflict with this internalised rule. His id was driven to derive sexual pleasure from other men.

Culture, community, religion, media, teachers and peers can also shape someone's superego. For Nigel, it is likely that his parents' view on the way of the world was shared by many in the small community. Nigel was surrounded by this belief. Nigel attended Sunday school and chapel and this too can expose a child to a very clear set of rules for living. For example, in the discussion of Bible stories but also in a very concrete way with the introduction of the Ten Commandments. We are aware that still, in some religious communities today, homosexuality is not accepted by its members. With regard to media exposure, Nigel explained how the accepted gay characters on TV at the time were portrayed as "camp" and Nigel could not identify with this way of being.

We can see how in other areas of Nigel's life, the anecdotes that are remembered are those that involve feedback from others that have shaped his life significantly. The school teacher, who, in that moment, benignly commented that Nigel should switch to refereeing ultimately resulted in shaping Nigel's entire career. Also, the bullying, the peer who communicated that something was not acceptable about Nigel despite Nigel not knowing what this was at the time. This in itself likely increased Nigel's awareness that if someone did not like a part of you or was unable to accept a part of you, then this would result in ill treatment that felt unbearable. As a result, Nigel would then internalise an anxiety or fear that showing all of himself would result in something rejecting and unbearable.

It is therefore understandable that Nigel was struggling to accept his instinctual sexual drives later in his adolescence, given his exposure to what was acceptable and what was not acceptable in his earlier life. The fallout of this would have been an internal conflict: the id craving sexual pleasure from contact with men and the superego telling Nigel that this was not acceptable. With internal conflict comes struggle, and if a solution cannot be found the consequences are significant for one's mental health. The most extreme version of not being able to accept a part of yourself, if one's superego is of such great strength, is that an individual may try to kill that part of themselves off. This could happen either symbolically in one's behaviour and mental health symptoms, such as a denial of sexuality with protests of "I am not gay", or physically by attempting suicide and killing off one's body and mind. This is what Nigel attempted to do.

Depression and suicide

By the age of 26, Nigel had a very well formed sense of what was acceptable and not acceptable to him, based upon his early experiences. His superego told him that it was not acceptable to be gay. His internal conflict led to him trying to find a solution and one day he thought he had found it. He read somewhere that chemical castration got rid of sexual urges and so in his mind if he did this, everything would be fine. He went to visit his GP, sitting down to share for the first time, "I think I'm gay, I don't want to be gay and I want to be chemically castrated." The GP, much to Nigel's disappointment, explained that this was not possible and being chemically castrated would not help. Instantly, in that moment, Nigel lost his escape route. A few months after this, having lost his potential solution to his internal conflict, Nigel attempted to take his own life.

One night, he wrote a suicide note for his parents. He didn't say why but he said that he couldn't go on with life. He left the house at 4 am, shotgun in hand, along with a bottle of whisky and a bottle of paracetamol. He walked around saying goodbye to everything and then walked out onto the top of the mountains and sat, looking down at where he had grown up. He drank the whisky and swallowed the paracetamol in the hope of killing himself, when in fact this was what saved him. The combination of alcohol and paracetamol induced a coma and the police helicopter located Nigel with heat sensors to find him lying down with the shotgun on his chest pointing to his chin. Owing to the positioning of the gun, the police did not know if it was safe to intervene and so they waited as the heat in Nigel's body became less and less. Eventually, they decided they would have to respond or he would die from hypothermia. He was airlifted to hospital, remained in intensive care for two days, and was later told that he would have died if he had been out on the mountain for another 20 minutes.

Nigel now believes that he will never forgive himself for what he put his parents through that night. To think that they may never have seen their child again and the hell that he must have put them through. At the time, Nigel did not see his act as cowardly but as something that would have made everyone else's lives better. They would have been better off without him. His mother, of course, disagreed.

Nigel remained in hospital for four to five days after he left intensive care. During this time his mother visited him on her own. She told him, "If you ever do anything like that again then you may as well take me and your dad with you as we do not want to live our life without you in it." She didn't say anything else and left the room. Nigel sat in silence and reflected on what she had said. He sat and cried and came to terms with the fact that this was who he was and that there were many things he could choose but his sexuality was not one of them. He could choose if he was a good or bad person but his sexuality was what he needed to accept. In that moment his life was saved by his mother's words.

Therapeutic interventions can take all sorts of forms and they do not always have to happen in the therapy room. Nigel's mother had delivered a very skilled intervention which she gifted her son that day. She had spoken directly to Nigel's superego; regardless of who he was, they did not want to live without him. She had given Nigel permission to be whoever he needed to be just as long as he remained. What was not acceptable was for him to not remain: if he did this then neither could his parents.

Bulimia, non-acceptance, and wanting to get rid

Nigel has not only struggled with depression and low mood as part of his battle with trying to accept his sexuality. He has also presented with other mental health symptoms that are symbolic of his difficulties to accept a part of himself. Symbolism is something that I frequently see in the clinic. Historically, symbolism was thought about by Breuer and Freud in 1895[14] within cases of hysteria and how external events determine the physical pathology and symptoms of one's mental ill health.

Mental health symptoms are not always clear in terms of symbolism, but for Nigel I feel they are very clear. As Nigel was struggling to understand why he was attracted to men, he started to attach shame and dirtiness to the feelings he was having. On occasions, he would spend hours in the shower trying to wash them out. At the time he thought this was all he needed to do: wash it away. Nigel was trying to get rid of a part of himself in the shower that he could not accept.

He thought that if he did not present like the gay people did on TV at the time then no one would find him attractive. He started to comfort eat and binge and this led to significant weight gain. Nigel now weighed 16½ stone. In this way, Nigel's binge eating controlled the situation by increasing the likelihood that people might not find him attractive. This is a common presentation with individuals that binge eat and maintain a body shape or size that would be considered to be less attractive by our cultural norms. Often, if there is a fear about sexual intimacy or emotional intimacy, binge eating and weight gain can be used unconsciously as one way of trying to keep people at a distance.

---

[14] Freud, S., & Breuer, J. (1895d). *Studies on Hysteria. S. E., 2*. London: Vintage Random House, 2001.

In this way, if Nigel could not trust himself and his sexual urges towards other men, he unconsciously presented a body that other men were more likely to find unattractive. By this point, Nigel had acted on his impulses a couple of times but felt "dirty" and "really bad" afterwards. It is at these times he washed in the shower for hours afterwards to try to wash the "dirt" away.

Nigel's struggles with accepting his sexuality continued. Once he had gained the weight, he consciously was aware that the kind of person he was attracted to would not be attracted to him. He started to make himself sick after every meal. No one knew; he became lonely and was living a lie about his sexuality. He lost weight and got down to 11½ stone but looked pale and unhealthy and lost some of his character as well. So, he decided to go to the gym to put weight on to look better. Nigel then got hooked on steroids and at the age of 25 he was bulimic, addicted to steroids, and depressed. In part, the steroids themselves made him depressed and short tempered but he was also depressed by the belief that the world would not accept him and he could not accept himself.

It may seem rather confusing that Nigel's story shares how he would oscillate between wanting to make himself look attractive and wanting to make himself look unattractive. We would understand this to reflect the strength of Nigel's internal conflict and the constant fight between the id and the superego. The id wanting to respond to sexual urges towards men and therefore trying to make him look more attractive versus the superego telling him that this is not acceptable and therefore binge eating and presenting his body in a way that may make him less attractive. It is unlikely that the weight loss and weight gain were ever entirely conscious as a process. Instead, it is very likely that much, if not all, of this process was unconscious to Nigel at the time. Finding bulimia along the way as a conscious choice to manage weight and his appearance is symbolic of Nigel wanting to get rid of an unacceptable part of himself. Washing it off was not successful so instead he tried to vomit it out. The process of making yourself sick is to get rid of something inside you that you no longer want to be inside. And notably when sick is delivered, it is a physical display of something aversive and disgusting.

For Nigel, he has symbolically tried to get rid of an unwanted part of himself through multiple means: chemical castration, washing, and vomiting. All different symptom presentations with the same underlying mechanism: a desire to get rid.

Bulimia has been a lifelong struggle for Nigel and something that he has struggled to understand for more than 20 years. I believe that Nigel's bulimia is indicative of his ability to accept or not accept parts of himself and it is likely that, at times when he is struggling to accept, his bulimia may escalate or present itself again. Nigel now works as a professional referee on the international stage and fitness is a requirement of the job. This can also exacerbate the need to maintain a certain weight and body shape.

When he refereed the Rugby World Cup Final his bulimia started to "sneak back" and he made himself sick a couple of times leading up to the fitness test. The following year he looked at himself and thought he had put weight on and the bulimia returned. In a documentary Nigel made with the BBC in 2017 for *Panorama* on "Men, Boys and Eating Disorders", he consciously acknowledges that he knows making himself sick causes more harm than good but he still does not know why he does it. The temptation has always been there throughout his adult life and he is constantly aware that it could present at any time. Nigel is right in his conclusions; eating disorders are typically insidious and incredibly difficult to get rid of entirely if they are treated with a symptom-based approach. For Nigel, however, if the cause of his illness is treated, he is much more likely to prevent the return of symptoms. Therefore, if he can accept all of who he is, it is very likely that his symptoms of bulimia will abate.

Transitioning into acceptance

Nigel has made significant progress over the years with accepting himself and his sexuality. His friends and family have been very helpful to this end. The first challenge was accepting and understanding Nigel's attempt to take his own life. Soon after he left the hospital following his suicide attempt, his friends took him to the local rugby club. Nigel was nervous. There was a group of four or five and his friend bought the first round. He went around the circle: lager, lager, Guinness, and … Owens, what are you having? His other mate piped up, "He'll have a bottle of pils." In that moment, Nigel and his friends laughed and that was that.

Humour had cut through the tension. Nigel could return to the rugby club and his friendship group, feeling accepted.

His next challenge was to share his sexuality. Nigel had attempted to take his life at the age of 26 and it was not until he was 34 years old that he felt able to talk to his parents and his wider network. He was brought up to be honest and there was huge conflict by not telling the most important people in his life. Nigel spoke to his mum first and her response, "I thought you were … I found some magazines under your bed!" There were tears and laughter and Nigel let his mother tell his father. It was difficult at first for Nigel's father as this was not something that he had much understanding about initially. He is, however, now fine, and the love and acceptance of Nigel's parents have been found.

Word then quickly filtered through. Nigel texted a couple of his friends and within two hours of telling his mother, his boss at work and two friends, he was receiving phone calls from New Zealand to ask him if the rumours were true. Nigel feared telling his referee manager. No one else had come out yet within the stereotypically "macho" world of rugby. It was May 2007 and he broke down crying and asked, "Am I going to have to stop?" He was told a resounding "No" and that the Welsh Rugby Union (WRU) would support him. The reaction was overwhelmingly positive and he could count the number of negative reactions on one hand. Nigel, in his own words, "felt the weight of the world on his shoulders lift". Symbolically, you could interpret that the weight he had been trying to get rid of with his bulimia was now lifted by the overwhelming level of acceptance that he felt in this moment.

It is not surprising that Nigel has developed into one of the best referees in the world. When we think about the task in hand, the referee is the person on the pitch who observes, manages, and communicates to the players what is acceptable and what is not. It is by its very nature an auxiliary superego to the players. What we know of Nigel by now is that this internal rule book (superego) and protest against the rule book (id) is incredibly familiar. His tension between superego and id has been fraught over the years and something that he has had to fight and attempt to manage. In a photograph of Nigel at the age of eight, he was captured with six of his friends and cousins on bikes. They had lined up to start a race and low and behold Nigel was there with whistle in mouth, ready to officiate in the race.

As already mentioned, the superego (or internal referee) has to find a balance with the id (impulses to seek pleasure, food and sex) to offer a well-balanced ego. It is possible that Nigel's refereeing has facilitated an internal attempt to master the tension between these component parts. When describing what he has learnt over the years in refereeing he talks about how he cannot dictate and instead must facilitate and keep the game flowing. He is there to support and accept others having their own minds but to set the thresholds and rules of what is acceptable. He describes how the easy part of refereeing is to blow the whistle, the hard part is to know when not to. In other words, it's very easy to be a punitive superego, bashing players (or oneself) with the rule book but what is much harder is balancing the demands of the rules against the need to let the game (or life) flow.

Historically, Nigel's superego could be described as incredibly punitive and non-accepting. This led to his suicide attempt. Nigel needed to punish himself as his superego could not accept who he was. In a House of Rugby podcast, former player James Haskell describes how in the early days, Nigel used to have an "unbelievable death stare" on the field. James joked that he was made to question why Nigel was looking at him as if James had just burnt all his Christmas presents! As Nigel transitioned into acceptance, however, his friends and the people around him responded with humour and it is likely that this allowed Nigel to internalise a somewhat softer superego. A different part of Nigel's personality structure was strengthened as a result: his use of humour. In therapy, when we are confronted with an individual who has a very punitive superego, humour can be an incredibly important tool to draw on to start to develop a different way of relating to oneself. Nigel's earlier stand-up career likely helped him to this end and, as time has passed and he has become more accepting, it is now his witticisms that he has become so well known for on the pitch. He has become a very fair, yet humorous, referee: "I'm straighter than that." "You don't need to call me sir, I'm from West Wales."

Nigel in part, also credits this to the environment and culture in which he has developed. He describes how rugby is one of the most respectful games and that it offers a nice world to be a part of. Nigel always treats everyone on the field with respect. The minority has a bigger voice in football, but in rugby, spectators from different teams can sit side by side, everyone is respected and accepted. He has also had exposure to other helpful mentors that have allowed kindness and something softer to be internalised. His mentor, Derek Bevan, helpfully advised that as a referee, you will always make mistakes and that it is impossible not to make them. If you make a mistake during a game, you have to move on otherwise this will affect performance. Nigel now accepts how important it is to be human. To smile, to use humour, and to apologise, "Sorry, I got that wrong." Ultimately, he now knows that it is most important to judge people on the content of their character and he is at peace with knowing that he is a good person regardless of any other defining features that others may judge him on.

Acceptance and relationships

Acceptance is found when we are able to form a balanced appraisal of ourselves. There is an acknowledgement that there are parts of us that we like and which are inherently good and parts of us that we do not like and may not be as welcomed. By having awareness, integrating and accepting both the good and the bad, we can reach a position where we can relate to ourselves with a healthy level of acceptance of being "good enough".

Nigel's move to accepting himself happened later on in his life. There is a familiar saying in common parlance that until you can love yourself, you cannot love another. As much as I have an aversion to popular psychology quotes, the theory suggests that there is some substance to this saying. Until you can accept yourself and who you truly are, you will limit the degree of connection that you can create with another. Distance limits connection, intimacy and exposure of the individual in relationships if self-acceptance has not been found. One very common way of doing this is through finding occupations that require long-distance travel or unconventional working patterns. Historically, for Nigel, being an international referee has required prolonged travel to faraway places and this has likely prevented the most intimate of connections from forming.

The future

In the past, Nigel has been asked if he would change anything in his life, and he has commented that he would have given up the refereeing and his career if he could have had a nice quiet normal life with a wife and a couple of kids. He thinks life probably would have been a lot easier. Nigel has fallen in love a couple of times but has spoken in the past about his fears of being alone and whether he will ever be accepted for who he truly is.

My work with Nigel took place during the unprecedented time of the coronavirus pandemic in March 2020 and the associated government restrictions on movement and travel. In July 2020, Nigel was living at home with his partner at his smallholding, unable to travel, which has allowed for something different and more intimate to be developed. Noticeably, Nigel's Instagram feed had started to change. His followers were no longer observing images of rugby and his work. Instead, we were seeing pictures of his 40 pedigree Hereford cattle, farming, and his life at home with his partner and his dogs. This was quite the tidal change! The pandemic had enforced an opportunity for Nigel to show more of himself to his partner and to the world. Something, no doubt, which he feared but which has, in reality, communicated to him that it is both possible and satisfying.

As I watched Nigel's Instagram stream change, it appeared that now more than ever, he was starting to reintegrate those parts of his early development that he valued: his Welsh heritage, his farming roots, and his sense of humour. Covid-19 did something fascinating to the sporting population as a whole. At the clinic, I started to recognise that for the first time a pause had been enforced. The thing that is feared by so many athletes. *Who am I going to be once I retire? What if I get injured and can no longer play?* Covid-19 and lockdown meant that these questions had to be explored. For the first time, curiosity and exploration were flourishing and it was actually quite enjoyable! Whether or not the individual was at the point of retirement or injury became irrelevant. What was important was that when the time was right to return to training, they were no longer anxious about the day when it would all end.

I am well aware that Nigel is a favourite in the rugby world and thousands would be disappointed to hear of his retirement. In an interview in 2018 with Colin Murray on BBC Radio 5 Live, he spoke of how he has been refereeing for more than 30 years and it scared him to think about stopping. He believed that he still had the appetite, fitness and ability to continue. He referenced 2020 as the year where he may sit down and think about retirement and hanging his boots up. When asked what would be next, Nigel responded by saying "personal happiness" and keeping busy all the time because if he were not busy he may start to worry about the void. I believe that at the time of the interview, Nigel was single.

I don't know if lockdown will result in imminent retirement for Nigel but I do hope that when it does occur, he will not only be able to accept, but find real pleasure in being able to integrate all the parts of who he is. To find ultimate satisfaction in knowing that he may not be following society's current conventional path, but that this is absolutely acceptable and in fact should be celebrated and enjoyed.

Summary

For many a high-performance athlete, certain personality traits are skewed to the right: obsessionality, masochism, focus and aggression. For acceptance and internal worth, it is possible that lower levels, or a skew to the left, may be found instead. Low levels of acceptance and internal worth increases a person's vulnerability as they may never feel good enough. This then means that they will likely seek feedback from their external environment to confirm that they are valued and successful. This can result in individuals striving for more or attempting to prove something in their sporting performance. This is often found as a motivator that drives people to success; however, this can result in punitive superegos, never feeling good enough and eventually internal conflict and distress being displayed in mental health symptoms that are symbolic of this struggle. It is important that those in charge of high-performance sportspeople—our coaches, managers and support teams—are aware of this being a possible motivator that drives success and the associated vulnerability and risk. Additional psychological support will likely be helpful for the sportsperson to foster a healthier relationship to motivation and performance.

Part IV

Vulnerability

CHAPTER 7

Injury and retirement

One area that many sportspeople have been more open about has been their struggles at the point of injury and/or retirement. Perhaps this phenomenon is attributable to the fact that many no longer fear the impact of sharing their vulnerabilities and mental health struggles as they are no longer dependent upon presenting in a certain way to guarantee their selection to compete or be a member of a team. Throughout this book project, I have repeatedly spoken with sportspeople who fear speaking about their difficulties while they are still required to perform in case this may impact upon their selection or how their coaches and teammates will see them. The increased number of sportspeople talking about their experiences after retirement or injury may also be attributable to the sheer number of sportspeople struggling at this point in their careers.

Retirement and injury are not just points of vulnerability for sportspeople but for all of us. We therefore need to explore why it is that so many sportspeople struggle with retirement with such magnitude and present with symptoms of mental illness for the first time in their lives. In this chapter I hope to explore what factors may put our sportspeople at significant risk of suffering from mental ill health at the point of injury or retirement. As already referred to in the chapter on obsessionality, we now have a better understanding of the biology surrounding exercise and the impact on our dopamine system and habit formation. The very fact that our athletes have increased exposure to dopamine through intense training over many years may mean that injury and retirement leaves them vulnerable to developing depression as the pleasurable effects of dopamine release experienced secondary to exercise are no longer found. As acknowledged earlier in the book, though, this cannot be the only factor attributable to one's struggle after injury or retirement. To help me explore the additional contributing factors I met with Jack Rutter, England cerebral palsy football captain.

Jack's story

Jack was 26 when I met with him at his family home in Gloucester. I was greeted at the door by a solid, rather playful and energetic six-month-old bulldog, Roley. Also at the house was Jack's mother, his brother Harry, and his brother's support worker. It had been approximately six months since Jack had captained the England cerebral palsy football team at the Paralympics in Rio de Janeiro in September 2016, and this wasn't far from his mind as something he was coming down from. Jack had just returned from delivering a motivational talk at a local primary school and he had not eaten. I suggested that he have his lunch before we chat and later he told me he was thankful of this as regular meals are important for him to maintain his cognitive functioning further to a brain injury sustained when he was 18 years of age. We sat on the sofa together and Jack explained that he had positioned himself to ensure that he faced me head-on during the interview to ensure that he could hear me properly. Later he would share more details of his head injury and how, following an unprovoked attack when out one evening with friends, he sustained a fractured skull in two places and his cochlear nerve was completely severed.

I first heard Jack talk about his brain injury at a Headway Awards dinner in London. Headway is a UK-wide brain injury charity that Jack is now an ambassador for. I was taken with how Jack had presented such a positive story on stage, talking about his recovery and adjustment. I understood that Jack's presentation was fitting for the context we were in at the time, but I wanted to find out more about his experience.

Jack agreed to tell me more and confirmed that for much of the media and motivational talks, he often does not talk about the more challenging aspects of his story. We should start with what happened.

Jack had been signed to Birmingham City Football Club's youth academy at the age of ten, and at 16 he had signed a scholarship. At the time of his assault, he was playing for Birmingham City in the FA Youth Cup and their next game was due to be against Liverpool in the semi-finals. He had returned home for a night out with friends. One of his friends had just signed to Bristol City and everyone was doing well in his academy group. His final memory of the night was being dropped off in town by his mother and there being a puddle that he almost stepped into when he got out of the car. The remaining events of that night have been pieced together by what friends, family, and medical professionals have told him.

Jack now understands that when he left a nightclub early in the morning, he walked over the road to see a friend he recognised who used to play at Windsor Drive (a local football club). This friend was in a group of lads including one individual who, as Jack went to walk away, punched him on the right side of his head, fracturing his skull and severing his cochlear nerve. This one punch then caused Jack to fall to the ground, hitting the back of his head on the kerb, causing his skull to fracture a second time. The front of his brain also hit the front of his skull, sustaining a frontal lobe injury. Witness accounts later reported that there had been some banter among the group but nothing between Jack and the individual that hit him. The perpetrator's defence in court was that Jack had called him a "ginger nut", stating that he had been bullied in school for being ginger. This was not corroborated by witness statements and later Jack heard that the perpetrator had, prior to that night, been given an injunction order to stay away from a girl that Jack was starting to see. Jack wonders if the individual was jealous. A year before, the perpetrator had been cautioned for breaking another individual's jaw. In Jack's case, the perpetrator admitted grievous bodily harm (GBH) and was sentenced to one year in prison. He was released after serving six months and was placed on an electronic tagging device for the remaining six months. For Jack, the consequences that followed for him were much lengthier, complicated, and challenging with lifelong implications.

When Jack's mother arrived at the hospital, Jack was going in and out of consciousness, was bleeding from the ear, was spitting blood, and being aggressive. The nurse told Jack's mother that he was "lucky" they were treating him as they initially believed that Jack's behaviour was the result of him being drunk rather than through a brain injury. As it was the early hours of the morning, no doctors were on shift. Jack's mother demanded that a doctor assess Jack as she knew that something was not right and four hours after his admission a doctor "looked at him" and "within half a second" ordered a CT scan.

The CT scan identified a brain haemorrhage and fractured skull and Jack was transferred to his local specialist brain injury unit at Frenchay Hospital in Bristol. Here Jack remained for approximately three weeks and his only memories are blurred versions of those people that visited him at the time. In his second week he can recall watching films on the TV and sending multiple sets of headphones to be changed as he thought they were broken. His nurse then checked the headphones to find that there was nothing wrong with them and it was at this point that Jack learnt of his acquired deafness in his right ear.

As the weeks progressed, he then recalls getting into a wheelchair to go to dinner on a couple of occasions and going outside but not being able to stand up. He also remembers not being able to stand in the shower and having to sit down. At the time, Jack told me how he was unable to process his experience and just believed that his injuries were like that of a physical injury, such as a pulled hamstring that would get better in time. He did not have a sense of the long-term implications. He told me he was not given any helpful guidance or perhaps he just did not register it if it was given to him. It was after his discharge from hospital, when he spent months resting, sleeping approximately 14–20 hours a day, every day, that he started to acknowledge how serious his injuries may be. He also recalls returning to his back garden where he had practised playing football as a child. Jack's back garden is slightly on a hill and he wonders if this perhaps contributed to his skills as a footballer, helping him to run after a moving ball at speed and supporting the development of his balance and agility. His return to the back garden, however, was a frustrating one as he soon realised how off balance, dizzy, and tired he felt. His frustration was primarily associated with how he could no longer do the things that he used to be able to do. Instead he felt "bow footed", as he was unable to balance on his right foot due to his ear injury.

After a few months, Jack's skull fractures had healed and for him, as far as he was concerned, he believed that this was the time that he could return to Birmingham to play football. No advice had been shared with regard to concussion management or future risks associated to possible head injuries while playing football. He therefore returned to Birmingham FC.

By now, his cohort of young players were being told if they were receiving a professional contract with the club. There were eight in his year and two of the remaining seven players received contracts. Jack did not. The club did not say that this was a consequence of his brain injury. Instead, they offered to support Jack with rehabilitation and to try to help him get a contract at a different club. As Jack started to train again, he described how he couldn't see the ball as well as he used to and he couldn't get his body to work, to move as well as before. He is now able to strike the ball with his right foot "quite nicely" but it is movement that presents a challenge to him. His ear would start to ring as soon as he started to run and it would buzz if he headed the ball wrong, in addition to feeling dizzy and experiencing pain. Listening to Jack, I felt shocked at how soon he was heading a ball after his injury given the risks associated with this. He stated that quite simply no one seemed to be aware of the dangers at that point in time. It was 2009. The Football Association (FA) has since published much-needed guidelines on return to play after concussion, which was released in 2015. There is, however, no formal guidance on return to play after significant head injury.

Loss

Before his injury Jack felt "sharp" on the field but now if he runs quickly, he can't see what is around him and his spatial awareness is not good, meaning that he is unable to sense what is around him. His lack of hearing in his right ear also compounds this difficulty. With increased awareness of the impact of his injuries and his newfound limitations, Jack trialled with Cheltenham Town.

At first, he lacked confidence in his abilities and worried that he may fall over or would make a mistake. Certain rehabilitation exercises did help him improve his balance, coordination, and spatial awareness but at professional level he explained how half a second in reaction time means a lot and makes a huge difference on the field. He felt and still feels to this day that he is no longer at this level. He was never really blessed with pace and so he had to be "on the money" with his reaction times. This, further to his head injury, was no longer the case. He had suffered a significant loss not only in his abilities, but his future hopes and dreams. At this point he was signed to Shortwood United which he described to me as being at the bottom end of semi-professional football. Furthermore, he had to face up to the uncertainty of not knowing what his future would look like.

There are a number of models of grief that have been developed over the years in psychology and psychoanalysis. When thinking about Jack's story, Bowlby and Parkes'[15] four-stage model of grief is helpful. The four stages are numbness, pining (intense feelings of loss and anxiety), disorganisation and despair, and reorganisation. In my clinical practice I find this model one of the most helpful tools to think about the process of adjustment with individuals that have suffered an injury or are retiring. Grief is the process attached to mourning loss and it is this very process of mourning that must be worked through for sportspeople who are injured or are at the point of retirement. To mourn the loss of ability, the loss of a role in a group or team, the loss of one's status achieved in performing at such a high standard, the loss of one's identity, the loss of the routine in one's life, and the loss of one's dreams.

Throughout this chapter we will see how Jack has experienced various stages of Bowlby and Parkes' model. When speaking with Jack's mother she talked about how she could see Jack work through these stages and intuitively felt that she needed to be there to see him through. In clinical practice and within Jack's story, it is important to acknowledge how this is not necessarily a linear process which must be worked through one stage at a time. My experience has shown me that many of those working through adjustment tend to oscillate back and forth between the stages and can at times be in one stage in

---

[15] Bowlby, J., & Parkes, C. M. (1970). Separation and loss within the family. In: E. J. Anthony & C. Koupernik (Eds.), *The Child in His Family: International Yearbook of Child* Psychiatry and Allied Professions (pp. 197–216). New York: John Wiley.

relation to one part of their recovery and in another stage in relation to another part of their recovery. Each person's trajectory is different and of course some may get stuck in one stage and struggle to move to the point of acceptance and to be able to return to a meaningful life without intervention. Excessive repression (avoidance) can be harmful and so too can obsessive reflection which can lead to chronic grief and depression. Bowlby and Parkes state that the ideal balance between avoidance and confrontation enables a gradual coming to terms with a loss that can foster maturity and personal growth.

Challenges to stability

It was at the point when Jack felt that he couldn't play football anymore that he thinks he started to experience symptoms of mental illness. I wonder if this was Jack experiencing disorganisation and despair. It was a year after his injury, at the age of 19, when he recalls asking his mother to start the process of filling in his retirement papers. On reflection, Jack told me that he just wanted to be told, "You've had a serious head injury, Jack, it will take you two years, just do your training." He wanted some help or guidance or for someone to tell him what to do. He now wishes that he had waited two years before retiring. Instead, he left after one year with a mindset where he just had to move on and get a job. Despite attempting to do this he was unable to get a job anywhere. He tried at a local department store and at the local supermarket with no success. When training at Birmingham FC, discussions were had with Joe and Michelle who looked after him at the time in a home stay. They had considered possible backup career options if he did not receive a contract to play professionally. Options had included the police, coaching football, the fire brigade, or serving in the armed forces. Despite having these fallback plans, the limitations sustained from his brain injury meant that all these options, with exception of coaching, had now also been lost. Jack explained, for example, that he would not be able to work for the fire brigade as he can no longer locate sound accurately.

Another challenge was that of people in his local community constantly asking what had happened, or alternatively people knowing his story and not knowing what to say to him given that he had just lost his life as a professional footballer. Others, he told me, just didn't understand as he wasn't "hobbling around" or didn't have an obvious physical injury. His difficulties relate primarily to his balance, vision, hearing, and spatial awareness. He finds it easier to run around a chair than to walk around it and initially it felt like he was looking at the world as if it was an optical illusion, not knowing quite where objects actually were. This has improved but he does at times feel clumsy and when he doesn't train or feels nervous his symptoms worsen. In contrast to this, when he has eaten and slept well and feels confident, he can do most things on the pitch.

Jack spoke about the sense of isolation he felt with the lack of support he received post-discharge from hospital. He is able to speak about his injury now, eight years on, without getting emotional as he feels lucky for how his life has turned out, but he told me that when he looks back it was "absolutely terrible". At the time, he no longer wanted to be alive and he couldn't see a way out of his difficulties. He had no motivation for anything. Before his injury Jack would go to bed and dream about football, yet after his injury he would go to bed and there would "just be darkness". He was unable to sleep and would then start to worry about what he thought to be "stupid things", thinking of various eventualities for his future. He felt "horrendous". Jack told me that these worries still remain for him.

His current worries no longer include football, as he now plays for a local team, Lydney Town, who are in the semi-professional league. He also plays for the Paralympic cerebral palsy football team. His concerns now relate more to "growing up", saving for a mortgage and finding someone to settle down with. He is a proud person and wants to take the next step to earn enough money to support himself and hopefully a family one day, and worries about if this may happen.

The magnitude of loss for Jack and for those sportspeople at the top of their game at the point of injury or retirement is great. Internally perhaps these individuals, during the time they enjoy success, remain reassured by financial security, and for Jack specifically the potential promise of a professional footballer's contract would have secured this for him. The loss of this stability feels catastrophic and hugely anxiety provoking. It is of course not just the financial foundation that is lost but a robust identity that is lost too. Who do these individuals become once this identity is lost? This experience will differ for those individuals like Jack who lose the possibility of what may have been and those who did achieve their goals but have to retire through injury or age (which is often associated with loss of performance or physical ability).

For the individuals who did achieve fulfilment and then retire, does part of this identity remain? I *was* a professional footballer or I *was* a gold medal Olympian. Those who lose the possibility will never know what could have been, which can be much more painful and leaves much unanswered for the individual. Jack explains that he has "still got a bit of anger" in him and that it is "not good when the red mist comes". It is of course understandable that what may follow this amount of loss would be an associated anger and frustration that the future with its promise of sporting success, prosperity and security has been stolen. Jack's story does show how he has been able to use his aggression in an assertive way in the service of his development post-injury. By channelling his aggression assertively into his recovery and rehabilitation, he displays great resourcefulness.

A sportsman's identity

The very fact Jack played for the Paralympic team communicates a level of acceptance of his limitations. For so many athletes, pursuing a sport in the field of disability sport after injury is something they are just not able to do, as it externally confirms to them that they are now an individual with a disability. Jack has been able to do this and continues to be able to do this. He also plays for a local semi-professional team, again something that confirms health, in accepting where his abilities now lie and the loss that comes with no longer playing at a professional level. For many sportspeople no longer able to compete at the highest levels achieved in their career, or to continue to attain the numbers in training and competition, this can be extremely difficult, and playing their sport at a recreational level is a painful reminder of this loss of ability. It is this that compels many athletes after injury, retirement, or deterioration in performance due to age or an increase in competition to select an alternative sport or to disengage with their primary sport altogether. Jack, on the contrary, has managed to achieve a sense of acceptance with his identity as a semi-professional footballer and a Paralympian, something that may be seen as a huge emotional achievement.

At the time of interview, there was no doubt that Jack was trying to create a new identity for himself, something that he could now be and would satisfy him not only financially but emotionally. We are reminded of Bowlby and Parkes' stages of grief and how part of the process of grieving and adjustment to loss is reorganisation of new things into one's life alongside that which previously existed before the loss. Jack tells me about his current projects and accomplishments and how he now works with people like Ryan Giggs and Sir Geoff Hurst being an ambassador for a number of charities. He is head of disability sport for McDonalds Better Play scheme. Jack also works for the Dame Kelly Holmes Trust as part of its Get on Track programme for young adults aged 16–25. This is a personal social development programme where he mentors adolescents who may have been through the care system or been exposed to traumatic experiences in the past. He tries to utilise what he has learnt from his own experiences to help these individuals. He has also captained the Great Britain cerebral palsy football team at the Paralympics and now goes into schools to offer motivational speeches. The experience of children clapping and smiling is something that he enjoys the most and offers some temporary satisfaction. He is, however, never happy and is always looking for and chasing the next thing.

When recalling his upbringing, Jack described how at the age of ten he often lived in a fantasy world. As part of this, he created a team in his head called the "Triple A Batteries". He wrote down the names of all the players and would go outside into his back garden and narrate and act out all of the team's games from each of the player's positions. He described how in his fantasy the team was made up of kids that had just started playing, who were coached from a young age and by the time they were 18 years old they were in the top league in Holland. He played every league game and every cup game in his back garden, writing down all the goal scorers on a piece of paper. This is what motivated him to practise as he would play it all out. It lasted for approximately four years until Jack was 14.

Jack was, of course, like most children acting out his ultimate childhood fantasy of becoming a professional footballer. It is no surprise that his team was called "Triple A Batteries": this could be seen to symbolise something of Jack's persistence and energy with which he keeps going, chasing the next thing. Jack tells me that he never feels satisfied and that this can be a double-edged sword for him in that it is one of his biggest motivating factors but it can also mean he is always chasing the next thing and is never able to fully celebrate his achievements. When the GB CP team came fifth in the Paralympics and they didn't get a medal, he knew he was not going to be happy until they won a medal. I asked if this would then satisfy him. He was uncertain.

This reminds us that for high-performance athletes, the underlying motivation that drives them does not suddenly disappear at injury or retirement. In previous chapters we have considered the motivational drive associated with obsessionality, masochism and focus, and for Jack the very thing that made him so driven and successful at his sport still remains post-injury. For him the primary driver behind his sporting success was his inability to feel satisfied, something that perhaps the external feedback and glory from professional football may have sated briefly but then spurred him on to seek more of, despite his achievements.

His aggression had also been a feature for him, perhaps again something indicative of how hungry he is to be satisfied. As a child both his mum and dad had "a bit of anger in them" and he too could "just see red and switch". I wonder if this is one of the very reasons that injury and retirement are particularly painful for our high-performance athletes as their motivational drive still remains yet the sport that allowed them to discharge this can no longer be relied upon. Jack may be a further example of someone who used his sport to discharge his anger in a socially acceptable way. I explored this with Jack and he confirmed that he would get as much satisfaction from putting in a ferocious tackle as he would from scoring a goal. It then leaves the question of what is the individual meant to do with this drive once they are forced to walk away from sport through injury or retirement.

In addition to this, I couldn't help but be struck with how vivid Jack's childhood fantasy pretty much mirrored his reality until the point of injury. Childhood fantasies like Jack's, which he was somewhat embarrassed to share, are anything but an embarrassment and are incredibly important for children to create. For most children, however, it is early on in their lives that their fantasies are sadly shattered. They are not going to be the multi-platinum album singer they so hoped to be and they are not going to be the astronaut or professional footballer they dreamed about becoming. This challenges the child's omnipotence and how they cannot do everything that is fantasised in their mind. This is an incredibly painful process but something that nearly all children work through and survive. It is a healthy developmental stage that challenges a child's sense of power. It also allows children to learn the difference between reality and fantasy and something of their own limitations.

For sportspeople like Jack who do not receive this early challenge to their omnipotence, we have identified another point of vulnerability where this developmental task has to be encountered much later in life, at the point of injury or retirement where they are no longer able to make their fantasy a reality. The consequence is a delayed, much more painful challenge to a sense of power and control in their life. They have thus far been able to do everything they have desired and now something dares to challenge this.

I want to return to think a bit more about Jack's motivational drive as Jack did wonder if always chasing the next thing impacts upon his continued performance and that perhaps on occasions it can be a hindrance to him. He has met with a sports psychologist in the past during his time with Team GB, specifically to discuss how he can get "wound up" and how he could relax more, especially on his days off. He had not, however, spoken with the sports psychologist about his anxiety. I wonder how the two must be linked in some way. Despite this, he didn't feel comfortable discussing his anxiety in an environment where he was the captain of the team, as he was concerned that people may have seen this as a bit of a weakness. He did, on reflection, appreciate that perhaps he could have spoken with the sports psychologist as he was not responsible for team selection.

Jack is not the first athlete to express concerns about sharing difficulties regarding their mental health with coaches or other sports professionals in the team. Many even talk about how they fear sharing their difficulties with their teammates too, for fear that they may go to a coach and this may jeopardise an ongoing position in the squad. My hope is that with this book, many may realise that it is these personality traits or symptoms that may actually be driving success and achievement, and in order to optimise performance and more general mental health and well-being it is absolutely this information and insight that needs to be shared and thought about in order to succeed in a healthy way.

What drives athletes?

Jack grew up the youngest in a family that consisted of his mum, dad, brother, and sister. Mum was available during the interview if Jack needed anything and it seemed that this was very much consistent with Jack's experience of his mother throughout his upbringing. Jack's sister is now a barrister. Jack's brother has a diagnosis of autism; however, the family were not aware of this until he was ten years old. Jack would have been five at the time, the same age as when he started to play football. When he was younger, he struggled to understand his brother's needs. Within all families, every child will take a role specifically related to the complex dynamics inherent in any family. I wondered how perhaps Jack's role in his family as the youngest of three was to be the sporty child, whereby sporting achievements would get him noticed. For his sister, perhaps it was her academic achievements that would get her noticed. Jack told me that he had always been competitive with his sister. If sport has been used as something to get a high-performance athlete noticed or to receive positive feedback that might otherwise be lacking, we once again can see an increased vulnerability at the point of injury or retirement if they are no longer able to use sport in this way.

Jack's mother explained that she wanted all her children to believe that they could do whatever they wanted to do and that she too would believe in them. She described how she found watching Jack's development in football "just beautiful", admiring his hard work, determination, and effort that was getting him what he wanted. She hoped this was not at the expense of other things like relationships. She wanted her children to be the best they could be and that Jack would always be hypercritical of himself but she felt that this was good as she believes it is "no good to sit on your laurels". She thinks that it is this pre-existing trait that also contributed to Jack's recovery after his brain injury as he fought to achieve more and improve. Jack felt this way too and described how he would instinctively go on YouTube after his injury to learn what he needed to do to improve.

Jack's father was described as being more practical in nature. He was "really good" at taking Jack to football and would also buy him football boots. After a tough game Jack would be his own worst critic and his father would just let him "mull things over" and would then say something "stupid". His mum was described as very emotional and his dad as emotionless. He shared that he had never seen his father cry or show any real emotion with the exception of anger. Jack spoke about how even before his head injury he had a capacity to "see red" and "switch". He believes that it was this capacity for anger on the pitch that prevented him from captaining Birmingham FC.

After his head injury he had been crying and upset in front of his father who did not know what to say and would say unhelpful things like "You shouldn't have been out." Jack was injured in March 2009 and by October 2009 his father had left the family home, at a time when Jack and the family very much needed him. I wondered if Jack felt that his head injury contributed to the divorce of his parents. He said he thought not. He explained that it had been coming. Times were hard for the family at first after the divorce and his injury, and especially hard on his mother with the demands of looking after Jack and his brother. Jack did explain that the home environment is now much better and more harmonious. He describes a real bond and closeness with his mother and sister. He told me that when he has his own family, he will not make the same mistakes his father did.

I sensed that within Jack there was perhaps a wish to repair things and to not become his father. I also wondered about the possible link between Jack's anxiety about having to provide for his own family in the future and his inflated sense of responsibility for his family of origin as the new man of the house subsequent to his dad leaving.

Later in the interview I was interested to know if Jack felt that his injury had changed his view on life, given the traumatic nature of his experience. Jack responded by telling me that he now feels more open-minded and described how he used to be a "bit cold" and lacking in sympathy when appraising the behaviour of others and when they would express concern about issues in their lives. He is now more sympathetic and gets a lot from helping others. Many footballers have reputations yet he wants to be the player that doesn't get big money but gives back the most, which he feels the top-level players should be doing. He wants to give back more and feels immense satisfaction receiving messages from children with cerebral palsy who have been inspired by his journey. He recognises that he needed help and wanted someone to put their arm around him and so he will always try to help others.

I was struck by how potentially his experiences with his own injury and all the associated losses, in addition to the loss of his father, triggered Jack's motivation to become more emotionally connected to others and not to repeat his father's behaviour. Freud[16] will talk about how instinctively we all feel compelled to repeat challenging relationships or experiences from our past with a wish that we may one day master these struggles. This is not pathological and is true for us all. Jack later talks about how he has found himself going on nights out drinking. Some, when reading this, may query how, after succumbing to such trauma after an unprovoked attack on a night out, Jack can do this. I would query if this too was Jack wanting to unconsciously put himself in the same position that led to his injuries in hope of mastering this psychological obstacle.

Jack himself wonders if his anxiety is an ongoing issue. On occasions he can get a "bit down" yet he is no longer depressed. However, his experience of anxiety is still something that can get the better of him and does frustrate him. He queried if this is why he now goes out socialising and drinking "a bit too much". This offers him some sort of "release". Jack perceived that he had "been a bit bad recently" when in fact this was going out most weekends on a Saturday. He hasn't got a girlfriend or a mortgage and so just goes out to have fun. It seemed that Jack was trying to reassure himself that this behaviour was OK and when I reflected this back to him, he confirmed that he probably was seeking reassurance.

I thought about this a bit more with Jack and shared my own thoughts on the matter. Specifically, I shared the observation of how many successful sportspeople engage in such disciplined, obsessive training regimes that follow rules and regulations stipulating how they

---

[16] Freud, S. (1914g). "Remembering, Repeating and Working-through (Further Recommendations on the Technique of Psycho-Analysis, II)". *S. E., 12*. London: Hogarth.

should conduct their lives. This becomes all-encompassing, for example with control around food, sleep, socialising, and lifestyle, that it leaves little time for play or, in Jack's words, "release" from these controls and parameters. In psychoanalysis we consider the developmental stages for all individuals and the developmental tasks for each of these stages. For adolescence the typical behaviours of protest, exploration, play, experimentation, freedom, pushing against boundaries, and rules are all incredibly healthy and are needed to support development and progression into a mature adult position. This also supports the development of one's own identity and sexual maturity.

With Jack's story in particular, and how it parallels those of so many successful sportspersons who start to engage in competitive sport from such a young age, some of these key developmental processes can be missed out on or delayed given that regime and control is the order of the day. If this is the case, we are potentially looking at many of our sportspeople delaying these developmental tasks and remaining instead in latency (the stage before adolescence whereby routine and order is a key feature) until injury or retirement, unless of course their unconscious drives take a hold of them before this time.

This is when we may see successful athletes struggle with a loss of control that may develop into addictions or risk-taking behaviour such as alcoholism or drug taking that may jeopardise their performance. It is almost as if their inner adolescent is unconsciously taking it upon themselves to protest against the rules and conformity required in sport, outside the individual's conscious awareness.

Alcoholism and addiction are of course not uncommon in the world of high-performance sport, as already explored in the obsessionality and focus chapter, perhaps given the connection to underlying dopamine pathways and functioning. With reduced reliance on sport, this may cause a collapse into behaviour that is probably more accepted in society at the time of one's adolescence. With Jack it seems that this late onset of adolescent behaviour was triggered by his brain injury. Listening to Jack talk, I couldn't help but feel relieved for him that this had been one of the consequences of his injury, despite the associated risks: the possible gains that this had given him in terms of his emotional development were huge.

The sacrifice of delayed development

Just one year after his brain injury, following his formal retirement from professional football, Jack went travelling on his own for six months as he could not bear to listen to people "harping on about things". Frenchay Hospital "went mad" at the level of risk associated with his actions. However, Jack's mother told me that at this time she felt that Jack's position was akin to that of a caged animal that was hurt and that she had to just let him go. He was 19 at the time and she felt that he was an adult and she couldn't stop him but just advise him on the issues that may present. Jack travelled to Australia with just two pairs of shorts and didn't know what a work visa was. His long-term memory and intelligence were still intact yet his short-term memory, processing, planning, and decision-making were limited with an increased proclivity to act impulsively. He just muddled through and went to visit a selection of "amazing countries", did a sky dive and a bungee jump, only to share these pictures on Facebook afterwards. It seemed that Jack was finally exploring outside the restrictions of the rule-bound past that he had experienced in his history as a professional footballer from such a young age. His next step upon his return was to go to university.

At that time, he can recall thinking that if he stayed in his local town, there would be loads of people who just didn't know what to say to him or people who didn't fully understand what had happened to him. Some people would refer to him as having had a "knock on the head" or would make jokes about him being deaf. He came back to see all his peers doing well either in the world of professional football or academia, and he did not feel jealous but this did hurt. He would also question what he was going to do with his life now. He was unable to get a job; at this point he was genuinely worried about what was going to happen and what he would do with his life. He would get "really down and angry" and everything would annoy him. He spoke of his isolation and sense of feeling that no one really understood him or put their arm around him. He couldn't really open up to his friends as they too just didn't understand.

In September 2010, Jack went to university to study sport, leisure, psychology, and education. Quickly he realised that he "didn't have a clue" what they were talking about in lectures and realised that his head injury had impaired his vocabulary, speech, and word finding ability. He was tired and soon found the course "boring" as he wasn't motivated. Jack didn't complete his degree. I queried what Jack's initial motivation for going to university was and he told me he thought if he had a degree he could move away from home and leave behind the problems that returning to his local community would bring. He shared stories of going out into town and getting into a few scrapes. He explained that people who knew the perpetrator would go up to him and be nasty. Since then, these individuals have gone up to Jack to apologise, having realised how serious his injuries are. University also meant that only some people knew of his injury. He had the space to explore.

Jack knew that he wouldn't pass his degree in the first few months of being there but he did get onto the university football team and engaged in the social side of things. He also met his first girlfriend. He was, for the first time, fully engaging in many of the social tasks of adolescence that had been missed as a consequence of the regime of youth football. With this, though, Jack spoke of how he was still a bit depressed and to cope with this he would go out partying and drinking to not feel things.

He told me how he became quite reckless and impulsive and didn't care about the consequences. He acknowledged that part of this was to do with a frontal lobe head injury (which can cause impulsivity) but it was also related to his anxiety. He did, however, lean on his girlfriend and stayed up at university to manage the second football team when they noticed his skill in this area. It was in this second year, however, that Jack started to experience panic attacks when coaching. He recalls visiting a school and not having a car or a satnav to find the location and forgetting children's names. He lost control of a group of 40 children and started panicking. Jack sat in his car and couldn't breathe. This was his first experience of a panic attack and he described it as "horrible". He told me that prior to this point he had not had time to think, and now he was only working a few hours a week, not getting paid much, paying his rent with his benefits, and had no clue where he was going in life and had no aspirations. He was going out a few times a week to suppress it all. He had a nice girlfriend and would go out with the lads but productivity wise he was going nowhere.

Jack's mention of productivity reminds us how for many high-performance athletes there is not only a reliance on routine, regime, and structure but a reliance on output, numbers, and outcome measures. These individuals then fall vulnerable to living in a world where they become defined by these outcomes, measures and results and that they become external measures of their own internal worth. For the athlete, being defined by who they are rather than what they are able to deliver is a challenging concept especially when years of performing yields repeated positive feedback through these measures. I wonder if for Jack at this point, a crisis of confidence was felt when he was just relying on himself to be, rather than to do and to produce.

Jack was now living in the moment; for the first time he didn't have a plan or any goals, both things that are so commonly attached to the world of high-performance sport. At the age of ten, Jack was signed to Birmingham City. From being in Year 9, Jack would attend school on a Monday morning to collect his school work and would then travel up to Birmingham on a Monday afternoon on the train, stay overnight with a host family, then train again on Tuesday to come home and go to school on Wednesday, returning to Birmingham on Thursday to train in the evening, then train on Friday again, play a match on Saturday, and have Sunday off. Jack did this for two years. He signed his first contract with the club at the age of 16. Living in the moment for the first time may have actually been very healthy for him, allowing him to let go of the routine and the planning that he was so accustomed to.

The fallout of this, however, was that over a long period of time, Jack was moving from day to day to prevent connecting with the reality of not knowing what his future held. He was eventually retreating into a place of denial and depression and starting to feel "really down" about things. It was at this point that he felt he needed to go to Headway. Jack joined Nottingham Headway. It offered him a place to go, somewhere he could be understood. One day, Jack asked if Headway knew if there were any disability football clubs he could play with. Headway rang Nottinghamshire Football Association and he was informed that he could play for the cerebral palsy team. He went down for a trial at East Midlands cerebral palsy team and this is when his career in disability football started.

At first, he did not know what cerebral palsy was. His medical records were checked at East Midlands and he was informed that he could play. He learnt that many of his teammates had sustained a brain injury at birth and that it was better to pass the ball to people's "strong foot". It was too late to compete in the London Paralympics in 2012 but he recalls watching it on TV and thinking, "Why am I not on that pitch?" The day the team got knocked out of the Paralympics, Jack was called up for a trial. The trial was at the team's new base at St George's Park in Staffordshire. He recalls driving up to the ground and thinking, "This is awesome," being reminded of some of the most famous stadiums like Arsenal's Emirates and West Ham's London Stadium. He was offered all the food he could eat and being presented with the opportunity to wear the England badge. It was here that something in him went "Boom, this is me." His confidence grew and with this he also joined his local team. Putting the England kit on each time, in Jack's words, "felt like something else".

Jack's biggest worry was being classified and ensuring that he would meet classification to play on the team. In the Paralympics, individuals must be classified and this will then dictate which sports they are able to play in. In Paralympic football his classification was mild compared to his teammates on the pitch and so only one player with Jack's classification is allowed on the pitch at any one time.

Jack's first tournament was in Canada in 2013 and he explained how it took the sports doctor three hours to classify him. This process normally takes one hour. They were "really looking at him" and his physiotherapist had to explain that Jack was playing at such a high level before his injury that this in part accounted for his level of skill. It is always a risk and a fear that you may get classified out of the sport. This too must have been a contributing factor to Jack's ongoing anxieties about his future.

On one occasion, when playing against Ireland, he scored two goals and could have scored four and felt that his performance was close to what he could do before his injury. Suddenly, at 11 pm that evening after the match, Jack was called to be reclassified and the team believed that he was going to be classified out. He shared how he "cried his eyes out" after just being given a new lease of life to play for his country and then it could all have been taken away from him. The team managers were "going mad" yet the doctor just calmly told Jack to go along and do exactly what he did before. He was classified the same as before and was able to continue. Ever since the 2016 Paralympics in Rio, where the Great Britain Cerebral Palsy football team ranked fifth, Jack continues to meet with the team once a month for training and for the first time in the history of disability football, players are due to get contracts and get paid for playing. He feels party responsible for this progression in the sport given the team's performance in Rio and this gives him a nice feeling and motivates him to carry on as he can now see things slowly going in the right direction for him.

Reflection

I asked Jack for his thoughts on his recovery and adjustment. He told me that he thinks he will never be totally over what happened but at the time of the interview he felt in a better position than he ever could have wished for. He told me it totally broke his heart. I wondered what "it" was and he confirmed it was the loss of a professional football career and the physical limitations he now experiences. His hearing loss is more of a frustration than anything else especially when sitting at a circular table and he cannot hear everyone. He has to compensate so that he can hear with his left ear. He still has moments when his losses get to him but he then considers how much he has achieved and more specifically how he has played for his country at the Paralympics.

Summary

Injury and retirement are challenging life events for everyone. This is largely associated with the losses incurred at these times. Management of loss, according to Bowlby and Parkes, includes a four-step process of working through numbness, pining (intense feelings of loss and anxiety), disorganisation and despair, and reorganisation. For the sports professional the magnitude of their loss at the point of injury and retirement is great. They incur the loss of performance, identity, a physical body that is in peak health, external admiration from fans, external measures of achievement and success, and financial security for some. The motivation that drove them to achieve in sport still exists within their personality structure and now they have lost the environment in which they could discharge this energy and effort. The athlete has to shift from being an individual who is defined by what they do (numbers, outcomes and measures) to someone who is defined by who they are. For many athletes, if sport has been their life, they do not know who they are other than "a footballer"; "a cricketer" or "a rower". They have to start to learn or create something new with regard to who they are, not what they are.

In addition to this, the early developmental task of having one's omnipotence challenged occurs at a delayed time leading to a more painful adjustment later in life. The child who fantasises about becoming a professional footballer typically realises very early on that they do not have the power to make this happen when they do not realise their dream. The child who fantasises about becoming a professional footballer who then does become a professional footballer will now have to have the bubble burst much later on in life and will have to start to adjust to a position where they do not have unlimited power and control to be and do everything they desire.

An additional significant developmental task that needs to be completed at the point of injury and retirement is movement through adolescence into a more mature adult emotional state. For many of our youth athletes there is the likelihood that training regimes and professional sport may hold them for much longer in the stage of latency (characterised by order, routine and control). Perhaps those that have had a coach who encourages questioning and pushback may be saved from this; however, for those that do not, the fallout of this is that adolescence is delayed and at the point of retirement adolescence should and will likely occur. Unfortunately, adults engaging in protest, pushing of boundaries and exploration may be seen to be more challenging given what is seen as socially acceptable at the age that many athletes retire. This can present a whole new set of challenges to the high-performance sportsperson who may remain in the public eye.

Where do we go from here?

When I was first confronted with the idea of how to conclude this book, I was uncertain. I hadn't considered that far ahead. A colleague suggested that the book required a refinement of the narrative arc. The introduction to the book started with my own personal journey, which led smoothly into the stories of others, but how would it close? Fleetingly, I suggested a final commentary on cultural shift or, in more helpful terms, a discussion around how sports culture can change. If we have a book full of people's stories that confirms mental ill health and vulnerability are present in our sportspeople and are potentially more prevalent by the very nature of what makes these individuals damn good at what they do, how do we hold this in mind, give it the space it needs to be thought about, and bring about change?

I share this anecdote with you, because it is important. The person I was at the start of this process, the young rower waiting on the start line fighting to win the race but not knowing why this was her aim, fell into the exact demographic described in my lightweight-rower research conducted some 15 years later. I was one of those adolescents who, as a consequence of my development, thought that if something needed to be done, I would have to do it on my own. The introduction of my own analysis, something that seemed acceptable to me under the guise of an academic training requirement, has, in time, allowed me to accept and understand the value of thinking alongside someone else. Something I was too stubborn, too narrow-minded, and far too defensive to accept when I used to sit in rowing boats. I wasn't ready. Yet, when my colleague suggested to me that we needed to think about a final chapter, I didn't hear it as a criticism; I heard it as a helpful suggestion. In turn, their expertise in this area and my newfound capacity for thought brought us here.

Where better to end but to return to where it all started? How could I allow this shift to happen? And if people are capable of shift and change, how may we support our sporting culture to achieve this? Well, six years of psychoanalysis, I understand, is an absolute privilege. Some of you with experience of therapy may be utterly surprised at the length of this intervention. For psychoanalysis, this is an average length of time spent on the couch, three sessions a week, for 50 minutes each time. In the NHS, you would do well to meet with a psychologist or therapist for 16 sessions of cognitive behavioural therapy (CBT). The implication: it takes exactly 16 hours to reach a position of relative health, or dare I say cure, to send you on your merry way as evidenced by the multiple outcome measures you have been asked to studiously complete during your journey. Sadly, it is not always this simple. It would be unfair and unreasonable to end here, to suggest that the only answer is for all our sportspeople to embark upon multiple years of analysis.

I recently found myself with some space; almost 11 hours on a flight. To have to remain in one seat for such a long time when travelling alone can test one's personality! What does one do with this time and space? Fill it with distraction of the most recent Hollywood blockbuster movies found on your free in-flight entertainment, access WiFi 37,000 feet above the ocean and continue to stay on the treadmill of work, or stop? It was in this moment that I picked up a book that I had recently purchased for my trip, *Why I'm No Longer Talking to White People about Race* by Reni Eddo-Lodge.[17] I stumbled upon a story in the history section of the opening chapter of the book. In 1982, a sociology lecturer, John Fernandez, was tasked with

---

[17] Eddo-Lodge, R. (2018). *Why I'm No Longer Talking to White People about Race.* London: Bloomsbury.

developing a course on multiculturalism for newly employed police cadets. To inform the development of this course, he asked existing cadets what their thoughts were on black people. What followed was shocking. Fernandez's response was not, however, one of outrage and resentment, which would have fuelled anger and hatred. Instead, he responded by stating that this was exactly why he needed to offer an anti-racism course instead of a multiculturalism course to "explain to them how it comes about that they all think the way they do".

I thought this was exactly the response that was required: to acknowledge the reality; to respond to something with compassion and understanding; and to think about why we find ourselves in the position we do today. If Fernandez were to go into that police training with resentment, bitterness, and quite frankly a stern telling off to all the cadets, all he would have got back was defensiveness, anger, and an inability to think or move. We see this pattern of events all too often when one group feels oppressed or outraged: they attack; and when they attack, their opposition responds in a similar way. This maintains the previous state of play and no change can occur. Instead, horns are locked and a position of stasis is maintained with neither side backing down.

So, what does this have to do with change in sporting environments? Well, how about we first take a leaf out of Fernandez's book and sit down and think with our sportspeople, coaches, and sporting bodies about how we have found ourselves in the position we are in today in a compassionate and understanding way. Not to attack and not to blame. I hope that if this book has achieved anything, it has been able to communicate the immense complexity we are confronted with when trying to unravel how we have found ourselves with the sporting world that we have today.

Sportspeople and people working in sport bring their own developmental experiences with them into sporting environments. This means that they will already have template ways of relating to themselves and others that they take into sporting groups both consciously and unconsciously. This can sit anywhere on the continuum of healthy to unhealthy and everything in-between. Each country also has an associated set of cultural values and attitudes shaped by history and so this will influence government, sports bodies and the sporting agenda from the top down.

The individual and group dynamics that establish themselves are, as a result, complex, challenging and unique.

Duty of care to date

In December 2015, Baroness Tanni Grey-Thompson, Paralympian and later a member of the House of Lords, was asked by the sports minister to complete an independent review regarding the state of British sport and to make recommendations on how better to support and care for our athletes. Her findings were published in April 2017 in the government paper, *Duty of Care in Sport: Independent Report to Government.* Tanni was happy to discuss her findings with me. To her absolute surprise, even people who held huge amounts of power and responsibility in sport were of the opinion that "duty of care" was not an issue in British sport. We appear, with some individuals, to continue to be wrestling with generational difference and outdated beliefs that duty of care is not an issue and mental health does not exist, or, if it does, then it needs to be hidden away and stigmatised.

The year of 2018 was a devastating year for sport. Multiple suicides of high-performance athletes hit the headlines. One that received much attention was the loss of Ellie Soutter, a British snowboarder and youth Olympian who took her life on her 18th birthday. Her father, Trevor Soutter, has since established a fund to support youth athletes. He has also spoken openly, criticising how much pressure is put on young athletes to perform and financially provide for their sport. Ellie's death occurred in July 2018 and in October 2018 another suicide occurred. This time the loss was of Imogen Evans, a 28 year old, who represented Wales at rowing and netball. She was two months pregnant when she took her life. According to the media, she had struggled with bulimia since university. I do not know the full details surrounding these individuals. I do, however, wonder that if the duty of care in their respective sporting environments had been managed differently, the outcome for these two athletes could have been so very different.

Eliciting cultural shift is a huge task and not one that will happen instantly. In the *Duty of Care* paper, Tanni has made many recommendations to improve upon how we support our athletes. I will not repeat the entire contents of the paper here but, in summary, her recommendations are organised into seven areas: education, transition, representation of the participant's voice, equality, diversity and inclusion, safeguarding, mental welfare and safety, injury and medical issues. One of the most important recommendations is the introduction of a sports ombudsman that is independent to individual sporting teams and bodies. This should be invaluable. I do not wish to provide a similar list of practical recommendations for change, but, instead, I want to think about what we have learned from the stories of the individuals in this book about sportspeople's psychological needs, and how we may start to think about triggering a cultural shift to support these specific vulnerability and mental health needs.

The British way of the stiff upper lip is slowly changing and we are now breeding a generation that is encouraged to have a voice, to have an opinion, and to not be frightened of communicating this, no matter how liberal or maverick it may be. Of course, this brings a whole different set of challenges and politically, as opinions become freer, the world appears to be at its most divisive. An article I wrote for *The Guardian* Opinion section celebrating Danny Rose, England footballer, talking about his struggles with mental health, seemed uncontentious. How wrong I was! There is a risk attached to sharing one's thoughts and opinions nowadays. Many a keyboard warrior can quickly displace their own undigested internal struggles onto the internet via social media in the most insensitive and grotesque of ways. Writing this book, I am under no illusion that everyone will respond positively to its contents. A part of me is concerned by this and fears what response it will elicit but another part of me knows how important it is for change to occur. It has to be done.

My primary concern is that when people pick up this book they incorrectly conclude that I do not like sport and that I am trying to expose something dark in a sensationalist endeavour. This could not be further from the truth. At times, after competing, I did not like sport and I did have a difficult relationship with sport, exercise, diet, and competing. This is not my current position. I value sport, exercise, and a healthy diet. Sport has always been a feature in my life, but what has changed is how I relate to it. I train around four to five times a week, always make sure I move during my daily life (given the excessive amount of time I spend sitting down due to the nature of my work), and I eat a healthy yet balanced diet. I can value the benefits sport and exercise bring to the individual, groups, and communities. The ability for sport to bond and bring a community together cannot be underestimated. Not only does playing sport bring health benefits to the body, but it also brings cognitive benefits to the brain. There is research to suggest that defensive martial arts can support development of inhibition skills in individuals with frontal lobe brain injuries and that team sports develop problem-solving skills.

To arrive at a different position and relationship to sport was a lengthy process. I have spoken at length to colleagues and athletes across all manner of sports and I was privileged to spend six years on a couch. I am now able to utilise a different healthy framework that offers me helpful boundaries around what is a healthy amount of exercise and food for an average woman (not an athlete). I also respect the need for my dopamine levels to get a little burst of activity every now and then. How each person finds this will be different and what is most important is that the internal change precedes the resources we use to facilitate this change. It will not happen the other way around. This is why so many people fail at diet and exercise programmes, because they purchase the slimming or exercise programme before they have done any work on their internal state. If you continue to relate to everything and yourself in the same way, nothing will change, regardless of what resource or tool you have in front of you. What needs to change is how you relate to yourself and the people and objects around you.

Where do we start?

Ruth Walczak is a lightweight GB rower who won two World Championship medals, rowing competitively for 15 years from junior to senior level. After retiring from sport, she joined a leadership consultancy working with business and sport to develop exceptional leaders and teams and has gone on to specialise in cultural transformation within organisations. Ruth has come into contact with sporting teams and sports environments and has concluded that intervention is complex. If cultural change is going to happen, it needs to be multifaceted and lots of small things will need to change. Intervention at a systemic level also needs to occur; working at an individual level alone will fall short. We agreed that the current dynamic in sport is one of "adult" and "athlete". The "athlete" typically inhabits a child or adolescent position: one of passivity where they are told what to consume, what to do, and how to achieve their goals by the "adult", that is, a coach or organisation in a position of power over the athlete. This difficulty is then exacerbated in weight-restricted sports where, cognitively, the individual is limited in the ability to problem solve and make decisions. Our brains do not function as well when we are in such caloric and fat deficit.

Ruth has identified a difficulty with mixed messages in systems. She can recall these from her own experiences. Within the same day, a physiologist told her to increase her weight as her fat percentage was too low, later to be told at a briefing that she had to come down in weight for an unplanned assessment. As an athlete, Ruth admits that she was highly motivated to row for her country and saw participation in the lightweight category as the way to do this. She feels, however, that there should be more in place to help safeguard athletes from their own determination to succeed.

A first step would be better communication to enable a consistent message to be agreed across all team members. What we know from so many a safeguarding inquiry in clinical settings is the importance of effective communication by all professionals involved and the catastrophic consequences of failed communication. I have worked with a professional football club in the past that developed their own well-being pathway, headed up by their sports doctor; the hope was that well-being would become part of the culture of the club. One action to support this was a quarterly meeting involving the sports doctor, lead sports psychologist, clinical psychologist, head of education and welfare, safeguarding representative, and HR manager to safeguard all players and staff members. Any care decisions made here were then cascaded down, with an appropriate boundary placed around player and staff confidentiality, and with an understanding that any risk needed to be communicated to keep individuals safe.

The impact of suggesting organisational change must, however, be considered. When I work with individuals in therapy, at the start of the process, I often find myself saying to them that things will likely get a lot worse before they get better. When someone has been functioning, running on a treadmill with defensive strategies firmly in place, as soon as the grip is loosened, things appear to get a lot worse. Whatever was being defended against starts to surface and things feel a lot worse and rather messy. This process is also likely to occur on a group and organisational level in sport. Perhaps this is what is feared. If we start scratching at the surface, goodness knows what will arise. And how can we respond to this if there is no adequate infrastructure in place to respond to these needs.

Earlier, perhaps the most astute of readers may have picked up on my use of language regarding the request for Tanni's government paper. I stated that she was "asked"; she was not "commissioned". Despite being asked by the then sports minister, a very helpful first step acknowledging need, there was no money and despite Tanni's report being written, the follow-up has not resulted in commissioning a working group to lead on the extensive recommendations. Tanni informs me that the uptake of her recommendations has been variable.

Tanni does not, however, wish to encourage enforced compliance. She is clear that the question we need to be asking is not whether all sports bodies are implementing her recommendations. Instead, we need to ask, are they doing it well? This was something I could relate to from my own experiences in sport and in mental health environments. Sometimes the provision of a clinical psychologist can be seen as a tick box exercise for people to demonstrate that they have one in place. However, this can merely be enforced compliance and the clinical psychologist is not utilised to actually manage any mental health needs. Many a knee-jerk request can be sent out from coaches and managers to "fix" their athlete to enable a return to play and facilitate peak performance but, ultimately, in-depth work with a sportsperson that is struggling may result in a position of health that reduces their motivation to continue to engage in their chosen sport. This is likely entirely inconsistent with the referrer's agenda.

Recommendations for cultural change

Simply parachuting in a clinical psychologist when one is deemed to be required will not elicit cultural change. Instead, a cultural shift, amassed by an accumulation of many small changes, will be required across all levels of sport at the governing body level, the professional team level, and within the coaches and the athletes themselves. Offering advice on this topic is another book in itself. I do not have all the answers and neither does any other individual. This will be a group effort where learning will have to occur over time. Having spoken to the athletes in this book I would, however, like to contribute the following to the debate on how we may be able to support good mental health and well-being for our athletes.

1. Changes to minimum competition weights

In horse racing there has already been a change made regarding acceptable race weights for jockeys. The minimum race weight has increased by 6% over the years. Despite this very positive change, physiologically, jockeys are actually getting heavier; specifically, 30% heavier. Therefore, the rate of change is greater than the sport's response to this change. However, horse racing is leading in this field and it would be heartening if other sports, such as rowing and boxing, would consider making similar changes to minimum competition weights.

2. Education

Supplements

If we can learn from the stories of Luke Stoltman and Mark Enright, we need to take note of how our athletes are supplementing as part of their regimes, and provision of education on this is required. Should sports doctors and nutritionists be educated in this area and should part of their role be to support and increase awareness in their athletes to promote a healthier relationship to supplementation?

Mental health awareness: recognition of need, understanding services and mental health professionals

Group education sessions are a fast and cost-effective way of increasing understanding and catalysing significant change. In sport, it would be helpful for every sportsperson and sports professional to have education and understanding of mental health, how and when to recognise need, what services are available and which professional should be referred to.

Despite being a developed country that offers comparatively good mental healthcare services compared to other countries in the world, I often find that the British public (not just sporting groups), as consumers, are not that well informed on what treatment options they have to support their mental health needs. Mental health treatment is not one size fits all, and as the NHS finds itself under increasing pressure with escalating demand, more and more people are seeking support in the private sector.

The private sector is growing, but it is a huge concern of mine that individuals with mental health needs are vulnerable and once the treatment door shuts, if, as consumers, they do not know what to expect or what is on offer, people can often be exploited or be seen by individuals that are working outside their boundaries and may not even be regulated by a professional body. Accessible information on different models of treatment, be they cognitive behavioural therapy (CBT), eye movement desensitisation reprocessing (EMDR) or psychodynamic psychotherapy, and information on the regulation and ethical responsibilities of mental health professionals should be made publicly available in one location online and in print. So too should information on the role, responsibilities and limitations of sports psychologists, clinical psychologists, psychotherapists and counsellors. There is so much confusion about the differences and similarities between a sports and a clinical psychologist and this could easily be responded to by providing education on the matter. A directory of specialist, regulated services should also be compiled of those services and support mechanisms already available to athletes. We do not need to reinvent the wheel if we already have people out there that are doing this work. We just need to increase awareness. As Tanni's paper identified, this work then also needs to be regulated by an independent ombudsman, in addition to each individual's regulating body, to ensure the ongoing safety of our athletes.

3. Access to a clinical psychologist

There is much debate on whether or not a clinical psychologist should be based inside or outside sporting teams. There are arguments for and against both positions and again I would imagine that we are looking at a question where one size is not going to fit all. Tanni shared that when completing her scoping exercise, she spoke to a number of athletes who struggled with trusting professionals in their team to keep information confidential. This was also evident in how many athletes did not wish to attend Parliament to meet with her and instead opted for an anonymous coffee shop in the centre of London for fear of the fallout of voicing their opinions.

For many athletes, when they sign a contract, there is a clause where they agree to sign over the contents of their medical records to their sports team. The boundaries regarding confidentiality and what information is shared with whom can therefore be very cloudy. Tanni explained that clearer guidelines around this need to be put in place. Some shared how an existing relationship between a coach and performance director was not disclosed and this felt like an absolute violation of trust, discovering that anything said to either individual would be passed between them. Some athletes shared with her how before seeing their team psychologist, they opted to see a private psychologist to prepare them for the sessions. In this way they knew what to say and what not to say to the in-house psychologist. For a treating clinician, this was extremely difficult to hear. The therapeutic space provided by a clinician should always feel safe, boundaried, and contained; with a clear understanding of when confidentiality may need to be broken. The boundaries can vary according to each setting but typically a line is drawn around any information that may relate to risk to the patient or to other people. Other than this, all other information is typically confidential.

Locating the clinical psychologist outside the sports team may offer the athlete a sense of safety and security. It would reassure them that no one else in the team, be that a peer or a coach, would need to know that they are visiting a clinical psychologist and that they are struggling. The fear of their position on the team being under scrutiny is eradicated. The flip side of this, though, is that it maintains the position that mental health is something to be kept secret, holds a stigma, and will result in your direct expulsion from the team. This should not be the case or something that we want to maintain. It is this attitude that needs to change.

The alternative would be for the clinical psychologist to embed themselves in the sports team and sporting environment. Perhaps in years to come, this may be seen to be more acceptable. To be seen as just another member of staff; another professional who is one of the cogs that make the machine work. Over the years we have introduced all sorts of roles in professional sport that are now widely accepted, the sports physiologist and tactical analyst to name but a couple. The potential value that a psychoanalyst could offer in team selection would be phenomenal. They would not be offering the same analysis as that of the tactical analysts but would be advising on who would be a good fit for the existing dynamics and demands of the team.

4. Recognising when something may have tipped over into something more unhealthy

Following the discussions with all the athletes in this book, I now hope that we have a clearer idea of when something may tip over into something unhealthy. The vulnerability that exists in our athletes as a consequence of their personality structures is also what makes them so well attuned to the demands of high-performance sport. Of course, this high-performance mentality is not exclusive to high-performance sport. It is a personality structure, one of being skewed to the right on a number of traits, likely inclusive of obsessionality, focus, aggression and masochism that may also be observed in other high-performance environments such as those found in the business world and in the military. Similar transitional difficulties post-injury and retirement are found in the military and the cause of this is likely to involve similar mechanisms to those described in the book. Principal among these are habituation to adrenaline and dopamine-fuelled regimes, an ability to switch one's thinking mind off to get the job done, and a power dynamic where one is responding to orders given to them by an external authority.

It may come as no surprise that consultancy services exist to support athletes post-retirement to help them transition over into high-performance business environments. This is based on the theory that the high-performance athlete has transferable skills and a mindset that is well matched to the business world: their business model is sound, and the personality of high-performance athletes is well suited to the pressures of consulting or the like. But, we must remember that this is just one pathway and athletes should not feel that this is the only way of functioning that is available to them, especially if they feel it is already limited or causing distress in some way. High-performance athletes need to know there are options post-retirement.

During their sporting careers and at times of injury and retirement where transition is required, athletes, coaches, and sporting organisations must keep an eye on the fine line between athletes using these personality traits in a functional way or in a way that has become pervasive and more clinical in presentation. The two key features of identifying something more clinical, for me, would be that of:

a. Significant impairment or distress in social, occupational and/or everyday functioning
b. The consequences of not training or exercising is perceived to be catastrophic or unmanageable.

If one or both of these are recognised, having a discussion with a suitably qualified and registered mental health professional is indicated. My earlier recommendation of education regarding available services and professionals will ensure that the individual or organisation is able to make a suitable referral based on need.

5. Fostering the adult to adult relationship

In science, one may suggest a hypothesis. On this occasion, let us suggest the hypothesis that "Mental illness does not exist in sport." In order to refute a hypothesis, one must find just one exception to this rule. Then the hypothesis is considered null and void and it must be accepted as such. In this case, the null hypothesis would be that mental illness does exist in sport. After sharing the stories of all of the individuals in this book I now ask that you, as the reader, are more accepting of the alternative hypothesis that mental illness and vulnerability does exist in sport. Furthermore, I would ask that you consider how potentially elite sportspeople are even more vulnerable to developing mental ill health than those that function within the average range on a wide range of personality traits: obsessionality, masochism, aggression, and focus to name a few. If this is the case, we need to relate to this population in a very different way.

At the risk of being rather provocative, what if we were to accept that this is a vulnerable population who bring fragility with them before they even step in the door of a coach's office? If that is the case, we need to relate to this population very differently. This vulnerability has been exploited in the past, and is being offered more and more coverage in the media in the present day. Contracts are reportedly becoming more punitive, characterised by loss of the athlete's control, clauses preventing the individual from accepting sponsorship from external agents and preventing athletes from accessing other income streams. We are now also learning more about coaches and/or other sports professionals abusing their position of power, taking the opportunity to exploit and sexually abuse their athletes. It appears that our athletes are vulnerable for many reasons but also to becoming commodities whose talent is controlled and exploited to deliver medals and subsequent financial gain.

The first thing, therefore, that needs to change is our entire attitude towards our sportspeople. They are individuals, not performing robots, free from emotion and their own thinking minds that need to be controlled. In the injury and retirement chapter we explore how normal maturation is potentially stalled in many an athlete as they are prevented from developing their own thinking mind within the more traditional relationships between a powerful coach and a passive athlete. We need to foster an adult to adult relationship in our athletes and coaches that flattens the power dynamic and includes the athlete as someone who can contribute to their own learning, development and performance. These are people who had lives before they came into sport and they are people who will continue to have lives once they leave sport. Unless, that is, they cannot comprehend the idea of living beyond their days as a sportsperson. Sadly, we look to the cases of Ellie Soutter and Imogen Evans to remind us that suicide in our elite sportspeople does happen.

We need to start understanding that, for some, they may still be potentially vulnerable adolescents who have an entire stage of development to nurture through into early adulthood and sometimes beyond. This stage of growing up requires careful management of emotional development, sexual development, and social development. In Tanni's scoping exercise, she often heard athletes describe how they just had to learn to survive the system. Both Tanni and I agree that athletes should not be merely surviving the system but should be nurtured and educated on how to cope as an elite athlete whose career will eventually end. We should not be churning out good athletes but good people.

The stories in this book have already started to explore what mechanisms are protective to the athlete and this includes creating a wider stable base with activities, education, and relationships outside sport. Acknowledgement of the need to support individuals with their emotional, social and sexual development is also important.

Tanni believes that funding needs to evolve to a new method which takes medals into account but also seeks to continually build the base of the sport. The era before the National Lottery, when there was less money for elite sport, actually had its advantages. Athletes were more resourceful and they also had to engage in work or other activities outside their sport which allowed them to develop other skills and abilities. More of an equal dynamic was created between the coach and the athlete. Post-Lottery funding has resulted in more money, but sadly more exploitative contracts, loss of control, and a dynamic between coach and athlete where the athlete is treated less as an adult and more as a child or adolescent who needs to toe the party line. This is then rewarded with greater access to media and team selection.

What Tanni suggests is an alternative funding strategy whereby all sports are given a baseline level of funding and then the winning of medals results in a top-up amount. If medal performance is not improved upon then it would only be the top-up amount that would be lost, the baseline funding would still be in place. This would mean that sports are not left with nothing and the model respects and understands that performance cannot just be exponential as one does not have control over what talent is available each year. Tanni believes that there is enough money in sport; it just needs to be allocated in a different way.

Sport is already making positive gains in more practical areas of need, supporting development of activities of daily living, like cooking skills and advanced driving for academy athletes. We now need to start to expand this thinking beyond the practical to the psychological and develop how we relate to our sportspeople.

Coaches and management must start to realise that they not only have a sportsperson but they have a human being in front of them, one they have an incredible amount of responsibility to nurture. If this is ignored, we fall into the trap of exploitative and neglectful behaviour where the person at the centre of an incredible talent and physical body is lost.

Coaches and managers need to start being trained in how to have difficult conversations with athletes about the reality of their sporting careers. They also need to be trained in how to deliver difficult news sensitively. Too many athletes have been dropped in the most insensitive way. Tanni shared anecdotes of team selections being shared in one big group room and those athletes that were dropped who then requested a conversation with the coach were told that he no longer had time for them. This simply is not acceptable. We need to foster a culture where athletes, coaches and sporting organisations relate to their athletes as respected adults rather than commodities. It will be this, along with consistent understanding and compassion for our athletes' vulnerabilities and fragilities, that should change the internal state of sporting culture.

Final remarks

The key message of this book is not to suggest that our sporting culture is fuelled by broken athletes. It is instead that our sporting culture is fuelled by athletes who have a specific personality structure with particular drivers that motivate them. Supporting athletes and sports professionals to identify, understand, and increase insight into these mechanisms could become their greatest asset. A successful therapy for me is not one that just equips a person with enough "coping strategies" to distract them and put a plaster over their points of vulnerability. Neither is it one that changes everything about the person in front of me. A successful therapy is one that increases the individual's awareness of their own internal world, both conscious and unconscious, and allows them to have insight into what their vulnerabilities are. Once this insight is achieved, we can then foster a new way of relating to these vulnerabilities and with this comes great strength. Having insight and understanding is our greatest asset. Our vulnerabilities are not something to be fought against, they are something to understand and be compassionate about. This should be applied on both an individual and group level within sporting environments if we are ever to start to foster something that is different and ultimately healthier in the world of sport.

Index

acceptance, 7, 26, 98, 111–127, 137, 139
addiction, 57, 77, 81–84, 91, 146
adolescence, 16, 28, 118, 146, 148, 152
adult to adult relationship, 165–166
adversity, 77, 86–87, 90–91
aggression, 59, 62–63, 65, 67, 69, 71,
    96, 127, 139, 141, 164–165
Akhtar, S., 88–89
alcohol, 73, 77, 83, 119, 146
alcoholism, 83, 146
ambassador, 94, 107, 132, 140
anger, 5, 18–19, 27, 36, 60, 62–69, 71,
    89, 96, 98, 101, 135, 139, 141,
    144, 155
anxiety, 39, 42, 88–89, 118, 136, 138,
    142–145, 148, 151
Asperger's syndrome, 76
assertiveness, 37
associative circuit, 82
auxiliary superego, 123
avoidance, 5, 93–94, 108, 137

Bako & Zana, 88, 90
basal ganglia, 82–83
Bergstrand, Michele *see also*
    masochism, 7, 55–72
binge eating, 21, 120–121
Birmingham City Football Club, 133,
    144, 149
Bowlby, J. and Parkes, C. M.,
    136–137, 140, 151
brain injury, 8, 83, 112, 132–137, 143,
    146–147, 150
British Horseracing Authority, 44
British National Formulary (BNF), 101
bulimia, 21, 120–123, 156
bullying, 60, 114, 118

caretaker self, 104
CBT *see* cognitive behavioural therapy,
Cheltenham Town, 135
chemical castration, 118, 121
claim, 38–39

clinical psychologist *see also* sports psychologist, 1–3, 5, 8, 25, 46–47, 55, 69, 75, 159–164

cognitive behavioural therapy, 42, 47, 154, 162

competition weight, 20, 80, 161

confidence, 15, 17, 59, 62, 70, 104, 135, 149–150

control, 3–4, 6–7, 22, 28, 43, 60, 66, 67, 82, 87–89, 91, 120, 142, 16, 148, 152, 166–167

corporal punishment, 95

counsellor, 47, 61, 162

Covid-19, 126

Cracknell, James, 112

cricket, 7, 83, 93–108, 152, 174

cultural change, 9, 29, 45, 47, 50–51, 81, 101, 153–158, 160

cultural norms, 28–29, 120

culturally acceptable *see also* cultural norms, 4, 24, 56

cyclo-cross, 7, 59

Dame Kelly Holmes Trust, 140

dehydration, 6, 45, 49–50

delayed development, 28, 142, 146–147, 152

denial, 29, 94, 98, 118, 149

depression, 7, 35, 40, 42, 51, 61, 71, 77, 83, 94, 97–108, 118, 120, 132, 137, 149

Diagnostic and Statistical Manual of Mental Disorders (DSM), 21, 69

diuretics, 22, 44, 49, 51, 81

dopamine, 82–83, 91, 105–106, 132, 146, 158, 164

drive, 7, 9, 44, 48, 74–76, 78, 84–87, 91, 98, 104, 111, 116–118, 127, 133, 141–143, 146, 168

drugs *see also* addiction; Lasix; steroids, 32, 80–83

drug testing, 44

Durham University, 13, 96–97, 101

Duty of Care in Sport: Independent Report to Government, 9, 156, 173

eating disorders, 3–5, 24–25, 67, 82, 122

Eddo-Lodge, R., 154

education, 50, 81, 157, 159, 161–162, 165, 167

ego, 17, 59, 64, 74–75, 80, 98, 116, 124

egocentric, 74

EMDR *see* eye movement desensitisation reprocessing,

Emery, Kieren *see also* rowing, 13–29, 49, 76, 112, 154, 156, 158, 161

enforced compliance, 9, 160

English Institute for Sport, 46

Enright, Mark *see also* horse racing; jockey, 31–51

Evans, Imogen, 156, 166

exclusion, 18, 74–75, 85, 93–94

external feedback, 25–26, 28, 102, 104, 107, 111, 116, 127, 141, 149

eye movement desensitisation reprocessing, 162

falls, 34, 41, 45, 49–50,

false self, 103–104

fantasy, 57, 88, 140–142

focus, 7, 74–75, 83, 90, 93–108, 111, 116, 127, 141, 146, 164–165

Football Association, 135, 149

four stage model of grief *see* Bowlby and Parkes, 136

Fowler, Graeme *see also* focus, 93–108

Fox and Beard, 107

freelance, 37–41

Freud, Sigmund, 56, 66, 74, 94, 98, 116, 120, 145

functional vomiting, 6, 21

GB rowing, 2, 6, 13, 15–16, 26, 158

Grey-Thompson, Tanni Baroness, 9, 156, 173

grief, 136–137, 140

The Guardian, 112, 157

habit formation, 81–82, 132

Hall, Eddie, 75, 90

head injury, 36, 131–152

Headway, 132, 149

Holmes, Dame Kelly, 63, 140

homosexuality, 23, 26, 111–127

horse racing, 6, 31–51, 161

id, 74, 98, 116–118, 121, 124,

identity, 8, 28, 32, 47, 107, 136, 138–140, 146, 151

immigration, 86–88

injury, 7–8, 28, 32, 36, 44, 59, 66–67, 83, 91, 101, 107–108, 112, 126, 131–152, 157, 164–166

internal value, 7, 26, 67, 70–71, 104, 111–112, 127, 157–158

intimacy, 120, 125

Irish Turf Club, 35

isolation, 28, 50, 58, 60–61, 70, 75, 138, 147

jockey, 5, 6–7, 31–51, 81, 161

Johanshahi, M. Obeso, I. Rothwell, J.C. & Obeso, J. A., 82

Lasix, 6, 43, 51, 81

limbic circuit, 82

Liverpool John Moores University, 46

loss, 8, 42, 98, 105–106, 108, 135–140, 145–146, 151, 156

Lydney Town, 138

Martin, Dan Dr, 7, 45, 48

masochism, 5–7, 55–72, 75, 111–112, 127, 141, 164–165

McGoldrick, Dr Adrian, 35, 41, 45–46

melancholy, 106

mental health awareness, 94, 97, 161–162

motivation, 19, 24, 40, 46, 90, 111, 127, 132–133, 138, 140–142

motor circuit, 82

mourning, 88, 136

National Lottery, 167

natural strongman, 80

nutritionist, 7, 20, 45, 48, 79–80, 161

object relations, 56, 60, 158

obsessionality, 6–8, 57, 73–91, 93, 111, 127, 131, 141, 146, 164–165

obsessive-compulsive disorder, 82–83

OCD *see* obsessive-compulsive disorder,

omnipotence, 142, 152

Opa, 77–78, 87

organisational change, 9, 159–160

Owens, Nigel *see also* acceptance, 26, 111–127

pain, 2, 5, 7, 14, 22, 28, 36, 58, 61–63, 65–71, 100–101, 107, 135, 139, 141–142, 152

panic, 22, 27, 40, 42, 64, 66, 68, 81, 89, 148

Panorama, 122
Paralympic Cerebral Palsy football
    team, 132, 138, 140, 150–151
Paralympics, 132, 138–141, 150–151
Pendleton, Victoria, 63
perfectionism, 5, 75
performance-enhancing drugs,
    80–81
physical injury, 91, 134, 138–139, 151
Piaget, J., 74
Pines, D., 88
powerlifting, 80
prisoner of war, 77, 87–88, 90
productivity, 148–149
Professional Cricketers Association,
    94, 97
Professional Jockey Association, 33,
    45–46
protest, 89, 118, 123, 146, 152
psychoanalysis, 56, 63, 67, 70, 98,
    100, 102–103, 136, 146, 154
psychotherapist, 1, 25, 55, 69, 86, 162

real self, 26–27, 104
regime, 5, 20–21, 31, 44, 79, 81,
    85, 145–146, 148–149, 152,
    161, 164
responsibility, 28–29, 55, 144, 156, 168
retirement, 7–8, 28, 83, 91, 105,
    107–108, 112, 126–127,
    131–152, 164–166
risk, 45, 51, 62, 83, 90, 127, 131, 135,
    146–147, 150, 157, 159, 163, 166
Rose, Danny, 157
routine, 18, 33, 41–42, 76, 89, 136,
    146, 149, 152
rowing, 1–2, 6, 13–29, 49, 65, 76–77,
    112, 117, 138, 154, 156, 158,
    161–162, 166

Rutter, Jack *see also* injury;
    retirement, 8, 132–169

sacrifice, 7, 14, 16, 18, 24, 74–75,
    86–88, 147
sauna, 6, 43, 48–49
seasonal sport, 83, 91
self-esteem, 3, 8, 25–26, 62
self-harm, 2, 47, 63–64, 67, 122
selfish, 59, 73, 84, 100, 108
sexual drive, 7, 116–118, 146
sexuality, 7, 26–27, 111–127
shame, 114, 120
social media *see also* Twitter, 157
social norms, 116–117
Soutter, Ellie, 156, 166
sports psychologist *see also* clinical
    psychologist, 8, 25, 46–47, 93,
    142, 159, 162
St George's Park, 150
Stack, Fossey, 32
steroids, 80, 121
Stoltman, D., 90
Stoltman, Luke *see also* obsession-
    ality, 7, 73–91, 161
strongman, 73–91
suicide, 118–119, 122, 124, 156, 166
superego, 74, 98, 116–118,
    120–124, 127
supplements, 80–81, 161
survival, 86–90
sweating, 22, 43–45, 48–51
symbolism, 102, 120

thick skinned, expectation to be,
    34–35, 50
transgenerational trauma,
    87–88, 91
Twitter, 107

unconscious, 17, 24, 55–57, 60–63,
  66–74, 86–88, 90–91, 100, 117,
  120–121, 145–146, 168

vomiting, 3, 6, 21–22, 48–49,
  51, 122
vulnerability, 4, 7–8, 16–17, 19,
  25, 42–43, 75, 108, 112,
  127, 129–152, 153, 157,
  164–166, 168

Walczak, Ruth, 9, 158
weight-restricted sport, 4–6, 11–51,
  56, 159
Welsh Rugby Union, 7, 26, 123
Wilkinson, Jonny, 75
Wilson, Dr George, 48
Windsor Drive, 133
Winnicott, D. W., 70, 98, 103
World's Strongest Man, 75–76,
  85–87, 90

Praise for *Skewed to the Right*

'*Skewed to the Right*. Even the title of this book captured my imagination and has been well thought out. As a medical doctor working in several sports over several decades, I have been confronted as a "front line" health worker to address many of the issues that Dr Amy Izycky has highlighted in her excellent work. The text has been eloquently put forward in this highly readable and informative book. The mental health and welfare issues of so many of our athletes are brushed under the carpet and as a society we have yet to seriously open up and address the harm that has been and is being done. Just like the government paper *Duty of Care* by Tanni Grey-Thompson, *Skewed to the Right* should be a compulsory text for any person working in sport who genuinely wishes to face up to the challenge of mental health. Dr Izycky addresses areas of controversy head on and this refreshing and necessary approach underlines that such issues should not be controversial because as a society we should be addressing them as mainstream concerns. Then we may be able to adopt good practice and truly demonstrate a duty of care. I for one will be a better practitioner for reading this highly informative, well-structured book. I believe that many more people who have been exposed to the idiosyncrasies and questionable practice in elite sport will say the same."
Dr Bryan English
Current Head of Medicine, Leicester City Football Club
Previous Chief Medical Officer at Middlesbrough AFC, Chelsea FC, The Lawn Tennis Association, and UK Athletics

'What makes a person exceptional in sport can also be their ultimate weakness. Dr Amy Izycky has cleverly combined storytelling alongside a more scientific narrative, based in theory, bringing this all-important phenomenon home to us all, in such an interesting way.'
Dr Zoe Williams
GP, television presenter, and former gladiator

'There has always been a fascination with what makes an elite performing sportsperson, but few have taken a deep look into what the cost of that might be. Dr Amy Izycky tackles this discussion with amazing detail and insight but also with sensitivity. If you are interested in truly understanding elite performance in sport then this is a book you must read.'
Luke Sutton
Former professional cricketer and now high profile sports agent

'Dr Amy Izycky delivers an informative and really interesting insight into the psychology of mental health within professional sports. *Skewed to the Right* is a MUST-have handbook to anyone involved in sports. Often overlooked within the industry in the pursuit of elite performance, mental health is brought to the forefront and explored in detail that really hits home and gets you thinking. The case studies and discussions she provides not only encourage you to understand the various mental health issues that occur but also allow you to identify and highlight when you may be tipping over or, as the title states, "skewing to the right" in your own life.'
The Mulligan Brothers
Inspirational change documentary makers